SELECTED POEMS

LARS GUSTAFSSON

SELECTED POEMS

TRANSLATED BY
JOHN IRONS

BLOODAXE BOOKS

ISBN: 978 1 85224 997 7

First published 2015 by
Bloodaxe Books Ltd,
Eastburn,
South Park,
Hexham,
Northumberland NE46 1BS.

www.bloodaxebooks.com
For further information about Bloodaxe titles
please visit our website or write to
the above address for a catalogue.

**ARTS COUNCIL
ENGLAND**

Supported using public funding by

Many thanks are due to the Swedish Arts Council
for providing a translation grant for this book.

Cover design: Neil Astley & Pamela Robertson-Pearce.

Printed in Great Britain by Bell & Bain Limited, Glasgow, Scotland, on
acid-free paper sourced from mills with FSC chain of custody certification.

ACKNOWLEDGEMENTS

This edition was translated from the following Swedish titles by Lars Gustafsson: *Valda Skrifter* (Complete Writings), Vol I, Bokförlaget Nature och Kultur, Stockholm, 1998; *En tid en Xanadu* (A Time in Xanadu), Bokförlaget Natur och Kultur, 2002; *Elden och döttrarna: valda och nya dikter* (Fire and Daughters: new and selected poems), Bokförlaget Atlantis, 2012; and *Etyder för en gammal skrivmaskin* (Etudes on an old typewriter), not yet published in Swedish.

John Irons' translations from *En tid en Xanadu* were first published in *A Time in Xanadu* (Copper Canyon Press, USA, 2008).

Thanks are also due to Pamela Robertson-Pearce for her invaluable assistance with aspects of the translation.

CONTENTS

11 *Foreword* by Per Wästberg

1
23 Fire and air machine
24 Landscape with one asleep
25 The balloonists
27 After rain
28 From a distant place
29 A boat from Murmansk
30 Episode
31 Conversation between philosophers
32 Happiness
33 The conditions
34 The dog
35 Picture
36 The bridges in Königsberg
37 A story from Russia (Metanovel)
38 Snow
39 Inscription on a stone
40 The machines
42 Discussions
44 Draft of a fantastic zoology
46 Bombus terrestris
48 C's monologue
50 Notes from the 1860s
51 The Wright brothers visit Kitty Hawk
52 Elegy
53 The living and the dead
54 Regarding the deepest sounds

2
56 Till Eulenspiegel's merry pranks I
57 Till Eulenspiegel's merry pranks II

58 Darkness
59 Concerning my relationship to music
60 Description of the Norberg quarry
61 Warm and cold spaces
62 Alba

3

64 XI (Sestina)
65 Sonnet XIV
66 Sonnet XVII
67 Sonnet XXIV
68 Sonnet XXVII
69 Sonnet XXVIII

4

72 Ballad of the dogs
74 Ballad on the paths in Västmanland
76 Elegy for a dead labrador
78 Song of the world's depths, the eye's depths,
    life's brevity

5

82 The silence of the world before Bach
83 The didapper
84 Poems from Africa 4

6

87 The eel and the well
88 Concerning everything that still hovers
90 Placenta
91 Winter in a Westphalian village
92 Old master
93 Austin, Texas
96 Elegy for the old Mexican woman and her dead child
99 Elegy for the outer boulevards
100 Elegy for lost and forgotten objects
103 Carl Fredrik Hill visits Lake Buchanan

7

107   Sörby elegy
109   When did people's mouths get wet?
110   Zones
111   Come tired body
112   Basilides' syllogism
113   Clocks
114   Audience with the Muse
115   The card
116   Berth
117   Aristotle and the crayfish
119   Variations on a theme by Silfverstolpe:
119   11 (Villanelle I)
120   16 (Villanelle II: An old barometer)

8

123   The small roads
124   All crazy small objects
125   How the winters once were
127   In-between days
128   Fichte by the kerosene lamp
129   Aunt Svea
130   A men's choir
132   The tired
133   Of course Superman is Clark Kent
135   Highly delayed, polemical attack on a Greek patriarch
       totally unprepared for such an eventuality
138   Traces
139   And die away like a storm wind in the desert
140   Minor gods
141   Letter from a joker
142   Lost property
143   Sleeping with a cat in the bed
144   Libraries are a kind of subway
145   Ramsberg's thumb
146   The girl

9

148 The hare
150 Events on the periphery of a summer day
151 On the richness of the inhabited worlds
152 Mörten bears his name with silence
153 The lamp
154 All iron longs to become rust
155 Varnish on an oar
156 Mirrorings and folds
157 From a hand-plane's recollections
158 The Christmas tree's visit
159 The prime numbers
160 Passing through dark regions
161 Through the looking glass
162 The meteorite at the Museum of Natural History
163 To the knowing
164 Trivial pieces of knowledge
165 Spring's joyous choir of birds
166 An early summer day at Björn Nilsson's grave
168 In a cosmic August night
169 Smoothness
170 American typewriter
171 Ramnäs railway community seen from the north
173 The logonaut

175 *Biographical note*

FOREWORD

Lars Gustafsson is five years younger than the Nobel prize-winner Tomas Tranströmer. In my opinion, these two poets are not only the leading poets of their generation but also two of the most important among living Swedish poets. And, it should be noted, Sweden boasts a number of high-ranking international poets.

How much poorer life would be without Lars Gustafsson's poems! I get that childlike feeling every time I open one of his books and am amazed at his imaginativeness, empathy and extraordinary divining-rod. His poetry has long been part of the family medicine cabinet for me and with the passing years it has, with its increasing scope and depth, become even more indispensable. I resort to it to find moods, states, impulses, echoes from my personal history, insights I know as my own but have never quite managed to grasp.

How is it that this aged faun, with his avuncular humming and friendly short-sightedness, sees and knows so much and still has the energy to feel so much? I have no answer, but open a book at random and read on that very page that 'man always wanted to be something more, have a face, a destiny and a sign', along with 'to have a soul is for a moment to land up under the cloud's fleeting shadow'.

Shadows hover over the depths of the world, dreams pass in an unguarded tremor through the sleeping dog's body, and inside the glass globe on grandmother's table a myriad bubbles swirl and make me think of 'the swiftness with which a great love grows. So great that it stands still'. His impressions pass rapidly, we just make out something for a tenth of a second – perhaps a winter scene in a Westphalian village:

> Someone has placed a bowl of fine porcelain
> over the ponds and hills and trees.
>
> At times this bowl is lit up from above
> and something stands out. Only vaguely.

The water of the pools is not exactly frozen,
but not exactly water either.

A state between states, where light
from a distant car in the dusk

vibrates, like light from the depths of space.
Far too ancient to maintain its wavelength.

At a bend in the road, a faint warming smell of pigsties.
Two wild duck fly up, purposefully,

as if the underworld were full of birds.

Out of everything and out of nothing the poet extracts gleaming spoils, neither fish nor fowl nor midway in-between but something strange that we have not perhaps seen before and that, like the burbot, that cannot be compared with anything else than itself.

One of his themes is that a human being can never be described in detail. That which can do justice to the unfathomable and unpredictable nature of a human being is 'a mysterious anthropology', i.e. poetry, art, a creative imagination. 'Nobody really knows what a human being is. Nobody knows who he or she is either. It is in that enigma that freedom exists.' But there are hidden pockets within us where we can exist completely and fully.

In 'Stone caisson', Gustafsson as a boy is prepared to avoid being discovered in order to discover himself the secret doors to the unknown. He gains a glimpse of what in fairytales one was unable to see without dying. He does not betray this but stimulates our imaginative power and himself gains an exhilarated freedom of movement. His find does not lead us to a solution of the enigma but into further enigmas. That no certain statements are possible is something the poet turns into a liberation of the imagination and a defiant acceptance of our own responsibility. Finally, the existence of the visible and hackneyed things of life is felt to be what is most enigmatic:

> My poetry has always been a separate zone, an activity with
> more degrees of freedom than the other ones. I have written
> it for myself and never for anybody else.

But his poetry has also been a research department where the rest of his writing has been developed.

At the same time as Lars Gustafsson develops memories and past images in his darkroom, he works just as objectively, with his clear gaze, as a registrar at the National Land Survey. Many of his poems are based on sober information from reference works. Penetrating analysis and reason are what he strives for, but he immediately runs into difficulties when trying to gain authentic knowledge. The unknown obstructs his path, in whatever form it happens to take – perhaps giant carp sleeping in the shadow of a bridge: 'They will always be there, those no boy can catch.'

His poems, half violent movement, half fleeting shadow, are borne by the intention 'to create out of experiences that have been made experiences that have not been made'. They form 'a vast ocean that, turned in on itself / fills itself with great mists / island by island and with no points of the compass.' Despite this, we make ourselves at home there. The cyclist from Frankegatan in Västerås may skid but does not leap from the saddle for decades.

Everywhere in Gustafsson's poetry one finds bicycles like some kind of domestic animal, in the cycle workshop a special peace reigns and early on he defined hell as a place without children and cyclists. In 'Variations on a theme by Silfverstolpe' we meet the boy who decades earlier goes out on 'a solemn morning' and climbs onto his bike, laughs out of sheer freedom and 'quickly and soundlessly steers with the secret away from us'. This time, the wheel enters a loose-gravel bend and he knows that 'the only thing I can do / is continue to steer / continue to steer till the end of the bend'. But the bend never ends and the cycle is the poem that Gustafsson steers wherever it wants to go – the cycle and he are one and the same animal.

I once talked about Lars Gustafsson with John Updike, who had reviewed him in *The New Yorker*. Updike had particularly noticed his 'digressions, parallels, proliferations and expansions, his way of meandering into surprising twists and turns'. That is very true. One never knows with a Gustafsson text how it is going to end and suspects that the author is not clear about it either. He is someone

13

who at every roll-call marks his presence from an unexpected row with such an indistinct Yes that the question arises if it was some other Lars Gustafsson, one of those who had been forced to add an initial to retain his identity.

But the recurring images reassure. And the 'limp, tattered train timetables that in some countries can be borrowed from the booking office' fascinate with their strange abbreviations. The poet notes departures and stops but does not board the trains. Instead, he is pleased by everything that is repeated – the yellow motor-coaches, the black dogs, the gleaming expanses of ice, the carpenter's bench with hacks and grooves, the unborn like a breeze through the grass, the fish beneath their own sky, the lock keys that open the gate to a childhood in Västmanland. 'Indestructible in the summer light, the mild meadows of the 18th century. And some kind of very small toad leaping merrily among the goosefoot. We used to catch them as boys. As one catches very small truths.'

Lars Gustafsson's poetry is a song to what has been lost, to the faces that are glimpsed in train windows and never return. Cultures and epochs swirl round each other like leaves in an autumn gale and attain a balance, if not before then in the smithy of metaphors that the poet keeps heated.

In the primeval forests and ravines he is at home, among 'tragedies, mix-ups, fêtes galantes'. The West is a living museum where Heraclitus, Descartes and Nietzsche and all machines, classical myths and modern information technology are linked together by a curator who does not omit secret passages and blind windows. There exist 'secret doors that you are not allowed to shut, that no one is allowed to shut'. On the other hand, there is no progress, for 'no development can undo the past. There are only days. Landscape.' He therefore chooses to disappear into 'the short summer of the imagination that was my moment.'

Knowledge and wild association, pugnacity and mystical absorption interact in Gustafsson with a speculative sensual pleasure and poetic passion. With his particularly intellectual imaginativeness he drills through the world's cement and turns it into a honeycomb: honey in each cell, but differing in taste. As in a game of blind man's buff, the obvious becomes alien. A gust of wind passes through a single aspen in the grove, but leaves the other aspens right next to it motionless.

And beauty alone endures – that is Gustafsson's stubbornly bold incantation in book after book. Often, beauty is awakened by the moments when we feel we belong to, are connected to all other forms of life. As in the summer night when it is 'neither earth nor heaven / rustlings far out on the boundless dark sea of the soul / a swifter bow through the water's velvet'.

In this poetry a defiance of the world order can be heard: 'Be in your own flight and never wait for the steps on the stairs.' The flute plays in protest against the battlefields around us: '...from the taut strings of the evening it sang of / all frost a thin and glass-clear song. As if / a rare love existed. We sing life / where there is none! And see how the water deep / in the well mixes the lights against each other.'

In a poem about Robinson (Crusoe), Gustafsson tells of a time 'when skills and tools / forms of knowledge, art, secrets / almost self-evidently filled life'. It was a time of imagination and free exploration; we then followed paths we did not know existed beneath the leaves. In the ballad about the paths of Västmanland he discovers beneath the visible writing of small roads the stubborn paths that know what they want and that have been trodden by everyone and no one: 'We write the paths, and the paths remain, / and the paths are wiser than we are, / and know all we wanted to know.' And just like the paths come into existence by being trodden, poetry is created by gaining body and voice in the reader.

The poet remains bitterly impatient at everything that has to be fitted into 'this great clock that we inhabit for yet some years of time'. But delight gains the upper hand, he has time to wonder at the carapace of a beetle, add dried morels to an Åland game stew, study the wrought-iron bridge in St Louis, share a churchlike warming fellowship round the machines at a laundromat in Texas.

So do the poems greet each other like old acquaintances who have not seen each other for a long time. The ideas dance over the waxed floors and the thought become seismographic curves that register quakes and displacements the rest of us seldom notice.

Gustafsson reveals a knowledge of evil that perhaps only basically innocent people possess. He has his subterranean cavities of coldness where he gathers strength and hoards supplies. He pretends to be familiar with all the tricks of modern technology, like children do when playing at being grown-ups. He can be seized with hatred and fury when disturbed in his activities in Austin, Texas – 'a small, peaceful place when I could be left in peace with my own business, and without reproaches. / I had been looking for something like this / ever since my first day in primary school.'

He varies a motif from Jules Verne's *Journey to the Centre of the Earth*. A vein of water ripples behind the rock face. Jules Verne's professor finds it, but Gustafsson lets the life-giving water remain inaccessible but close, like freedom. Over the years, he listens to and explores this true life that is right up close. This form of mysticism has provided him with an engine that is powered by unknown fuel and tremendous energy.

In the collection *The Balloonists*, there is thus a suggestive poem about the sea-fire that gleams on the night-time sea and the man who sails from fire to fire until he reaches the brightest fluorescence and, with difficulty, manages 'to collect a little of this water in a bottle / that like a strange lamp gleamed towards the cabin walls, / how the sea, caught, gleamed in his room with sea-fire / until the sheen grew dim and became darkness'. The poem seems to describe a distillate of the impossible, a shimmering of the elements along our fairway from darkness to darkness.

Lars Gustafsson is an Orpheus who, with each book, emerges from the underworld with newly gained alertness. He is followed by an Eurydice in various disguises, preferably red-headed, and he entices her along without having to take a fatal glance backwards. She is retained because the poem and the writing of poetry is never completed but opposes time in repetitions and new onsets. And she causes him to think of 'the swiftness with which a great love grows. So great that it stands still.'

Lars Gustafsson's oeuvre is an archipelago – from a great height the islands resemble each other and form a pattern we have learnt to distinguish on the map. But the poet unconcernedly changes shape and opinion and incorporates unexpected revelations with his almost inborn tone of voice. He reweaves his wicker chair, every osier a new weft in an old position, so that the chair continues to creak just as familiarly as before and even so last for many years to come.

More than most, he conveys a sense of an unforced joy in writing. He is a man of the enlightenment and an interpreter of signs, an encyclopaedist and a visionary. Knowledge arises and dissipates like twilight mist over Åmänningen lake. He longs for a magic that does not suspend nature, for a force that 'builds on impurity, mouldering, rust, ever-increasing amalgamation, ever-increasing multiplicity'.

Most of what influences us most profoundly – in Gustafsson's opinion – is 'a message from the gentle garden of pre-industrial Europe; we see the world in a rear mirror and no one has yet written the thoughts of our own age.' We can possibly console ourselves with the fact that someone else lives our lives; we are not to be held responsible towards the one who dreams us. 'Perhaps there was a house / but it is possible that we went past it / and never noticed where it lay. / We do not find the sure path. / The sure path is one that someone else found.' ('Stone caisson').

He wards off alienation regarding the visible world by competently cataloguing its phenomena. He pounces on old menus, reference works, books of physics, Sears, Roebuck's postal order catalogues. The deceptive precision of his knowledge stabilises a forward-rushing universe and makes us forget the danger of trip-wires, land-mines, landslides. The exact control and measuring instruments describe curves which reality, unfinished and chaotic, does everything to contradict.

He observes sensory details through the telescope of introspection: sharpness and distance at one and the same time. Åmänningen lake enlarges its deceptive expanses into an inland sea, an inner sea. At times, he is able within a highly restricted space – not more than a tightrope walker has under his foot – to express an unlimited freedom, a feeling that everything is possible if only one looks straight ahead and not down at the audience. Then a beauty arises around each hazardous step.

I am tempted to read his poems as secretive reconstructions of lost originals. What was written in passing on the ice and whirled away in the wind? Different interpretations uncover spaces that are then closed and become unknown once more. The real is merely a rumour, guesses, scattered pieces of a puzzle. Has he witnessed a shipwreck of cultures, taken care of its washed-up fragments and out of them created new compositions?

There are also points of rest of such a profound stillness that he can hardly have determined them himself; they lie there, like invisible beams, and do not seem to have anything to do with the author. And it is there, in the domain of the unfinished, that return, repetition and renewal execute their quick-change numbers. The poet obliterates his tracks so that he can delight yet again in uncovering them and returning to them.

A chorus of voices from past centuries, a book collection about to be scattered, the movements of lovers and the dead that seek each other, the kitchen table in October: everything opens up to an irrevocable loss, although 'they glow secretly with meaningless beauty'. And that beauty is charged with the memories of the larder of childhood: the winged corkscrew with its spindly legs so like a reeling brass soldier in the half-light, 'the beer bottles with their band of medals, all the signs of honour they have won for their goodness and brewing'. Writing becomes a resistance against the forgetfulness memory is so dependent on.

Distrust of blanket patterns of explanation makes his poetry concrete, physical and yet perforated with points of vertigo. It is skate-sailing on mirror-smooth ice, a physical experiencing of freedom in the glass-clear winter's day. It is the moment when the world is so close 'as if it actually tried to speak'.

The wall between word and world can never be pulled down, but in Gustafsson it is translucent. This is due to his exploratory patience and his courage to set a full stop before the poem is completely finished. His poetry is fed by a productive wonder at the possible existences that have not been assigned to us and by his capacity to keep all kinds of associations in the air at the same time.

And he succeeds in doing this because he does not tire, with boyish eagerness, of exploring the simplest of things, the trivial everyday life that 'opens trapdoors to labyrinthine and dangerous complications'. That nothing can be expressed with certainty he in practice transforms into a liberation of the imagination. We are our own discoverers, and a defiantly positive approach to life is concealed in the awareness that no one takes responsibility for us – that we must do ourselves. Gustafsson may play with identities, but he is not a relativist – he is a natural law philosopher.

He has a capacity – generously applied – to fetch comparisons from other spheres that illuminate or in a stimulating way confuse what he observes with his aged, learned child's eyes. The hollowed-out boats in Casamance lead him to the peat bogs of the Stone Age. He lands up in the peasant revolts of the Middle Ages, in the folk-song world of the Swedish pre-Reformation and he walks in the forests of southern Senegal through a pre-adolescent sub-terranean Västmanland. With an unerring imagination on which he relies with rustic obstinacy he turns every journey into a series of amazing returns.

In *Artesian wells, Cartesian dreams* (1980), the water gushes up out of underground pockets. Finds from what is hidden pile up. Moral laws and duty exist within us but also chaos, falls into the bottomless abyss, inextinguishable lust. The starry sky above us is supplemented by that beneath us: 'galaxy below galaxy in a never-ending well'.

When Gustafsson forms the frailty of life and the impenetrable pain of death, he criticises God's creation, but at the same time he lives in a pact with it, like a gentle-eyed animal in an allegory that only this animal – a Labrador dog – can interpret. Artesian wells are a synthesis of motifs in his oeuvre and, in my opinion, mark a high-water mark in 20th-century Swedish poetry.

If one reads Gustafsson's poetry at one sweep, one sees how it changes and yet remains recognisable, just as trees grow and age without our noticing it.

The lingering winter light over Västmanland has, from the out-set, veiled his world; in the later poems childhood is only a few days away. But the tone of voice becomes sterner, more intrepid; he is more himself now that 'proficiency has begun to become as thin as the dry skin of a dragonfly from some previous year'.

At King's College Cambridge, it is regarded as vulgar to have written more than three books, Lars Gustafsson – who has written about seventy – relates. But perhaps he has only written three and placed them in an imaginary library the blind windows of which are not opened until after the author's departure to one of his galaxies. Everything he has printed so far will then only be prefaces, foot-notes, appendices of this invisible oeuvre that casts a raspberry shadow 'firmer than stone' and against whose walls he rebounds like the bumblebee against the glass without realising where the glass ends and space begins. I think of this hidden work as a large animal inside which existence sleeps unperturbed. On a map its position is indicated by a sign that is not listed in any table of symbols, and the map itself represents a land of freedom, seriousness and play. The light falls over that land from the 'great Västmanland summer day / the stillness of which the child did not understand / and the expanses of which did not frighten the child...'

And now it is time, in conclusion, to listen to the melancholy music in 'Lapis niger': 'Now it blows through the grass, finally / It is late, and much has been lost.// Most people have gone home, and the summer is over, / and gates are shut and something is unfin-ished. // Fill your hand with stones. Fill your hand with gravel. / They weigh just as little as many days, // and that is what is inten-ded: / randomness and purpose coincide / but not until it is over.'

In Lars Gustafsson's poetry, however, it is not over. A lid is screwed down, it is late, but not all over. We hear him like the clear hammer-blows in the mist we are unable to localise. Despite this, he keeps us awake with his feeling for love and death and for the unexpected interconnection that constitutes life's adventure.

PER WÄSTBERG

1

Fire and air machine

An old-fashioned device –
it is driven by fire and air
the separate parts configured
so ingeniously that the water itself,
the deep water far down,
far beneath all that is visible,
in some way can be affected.

It is also called an air machine,
and one can carry out ascents,
or rather just the one ascent,
since the fiery air, the hot element,
slowly cools and evaporates,
while from a given point the machine
ascends to the altitudes

where the coming winters are formed.
And from those there is no return.
Its mode of operation with fire and air
also for short periods allows
distant days to be repeated:
summers before your name and your unrest.
It works slowly and makes muffled sounds.

– Does it let you see?
Its construction does not allow one to see.

Landscape with one asleep

For a long time he was in a sleep,
a land where white waters fell.
Its sound as when silver is touched,
and mountains stood still.
Who had been summoned to a meeting there
he does not know: no one was there.

He sleeps for a long time in his landscape,
and it is as water or silver.
Over the field the shadow of a bird is seen.
In his sleep he knows that it lacks sound,
like every sleep at once invites us to stay asleep,
each image asks us to remain within its circle.

Then the wind shifts and something is achieved.
The sleeper has seen nothing,
his sleep is the measure of his wish.
Of his awakening no one has anything to tell;
only a Portuguese traveller has recounted
how, far out at sea, the third day of his voyage,
from a point quite near the mainsail,
which the wind had cupped into an immense ear,
he clearly heard the bells of Lisbon across the water,
the gentle sound of bells above the swell's slow motion,
and how it then accompanied the ship,
till in a sudden storm that sail was taken in.

Now mightily that small pain burns!

The balloonists

See the tall man in the top-hat there.
He leans out with a gaze fixed westwards.
It's early morning, and the light reverberates.

The town with its clocks waits in the distance
the church spires cast blue shadows aimlessly.
It is completely silent, pre-departure.

Close to, the balloon is huge, like some giant pumpkin
that gleams and grows, it has many colours.
The hum of those who watch: a swarm of bumblebees,

they call out, wave to the voyagers in the basket,
who feign indifference, will not let on their destination.
They're motionless themselves and ready for their trip.

The man in the top-hat has still not ceased to gaze
and lifts a telescope of gleaming brass
as if he searched for clouds or something that's invisible.

When they ascend they will diminish to a point
until they reach the highest layers of air and snow,
the whitest snow that chills and blinds

will fill the air they breathe, will touch their foreheads.
In autumn it can be seen to fall as frost
the breath of upper air that gropes across the fields,

and you one autumn when the frost falls early
will suddenly recall them and their trip,
and how they still are climbing, dizzily yet higher

through a thinner air than that of winters
with a note like that of splintering glass
from forest depths of brittle rain

and how they rise yet higher through the years
until the very memory sings like thin glass
– and it is unbearable, forget me, rather something else!

A pleasure trip, a connoisseurs' adventure!
A gentleman, light morning-coat and bright-blue waistcoat,
that slowly makes a glove-embellished gesture.

It is free, already it begins to rise,
the cheering imperceptibly sinks down.

After rain

The sky of summer rain is like an X-ray plate
where light and hazy shadows pass.
The forest quiet and not even a bird.
Your own eye like a spilt drop beneath the clouds,
with the world's reflection: light and hazy shadows.
And suddenly you see just who you are:
a confused stranger between soul and clouds,
only by the thin membrane of an image
are the world's deep and eye's darkness kept apart.

From a distant place

Whether God or not,
whether meaning or not meaning,
at a distance the questions shrink to points,
at a distance shrewdness or fright do not apply
and free or not; there is action within me,
something acts and seeks out something within me.
If you keep still you can hear a sound of water.

It has to do with a darkness,
with living close to the right darkness,
it is like the sea beneath the ice-caps, invisible,
and only water-sounds and slow movement,
a distant sound of water, century-slow ground-swell,
and all your lengthy thoughts and decisions
traces that lead away and disappear.

A boat from Murmansk

A boat from the coast near Murmansk, extremely old-fashioned. It has high planks that are lashed together with horse sinews, there is no longer any sign of oars. A low coastline with creeping birches, grey swells, snow in the air. There are eight rowers who creep closer and closer to each other on the thwarts so as not to lose each other. The boat moves very clumsily, in a longitudinal direction. The sky low, with low clouds, snowfall, twilight. If we were not completely sure that we are on the boat too we would almost wish it were a dream, that it did not apply to precisely us. Which it nevertheless does, strangely enough.

Episode

In late autumn, on a clear and slightly frosty day in a garden held in the rigorous French manner, the philosopher Gottfried Wilhelm Leibniz is walking with a Bavarian princess. And he explains to this lady that it is a consequence of the principle of sufficient reason that all objects in the world have to be unlike each other.

For if an object exists, there is no sufficient reason for there to be a further such object that completely resembles the former. While this conversation is taking place, the frost-bitten leaves are falling one by one from the trees in the park.

And an officious courtier in attendance doubts the philosopher's thesis and rushes over under the trees to search for two leaves that are completely like each other. He picks them up from the ground and allows them to fall again, one after the other, once he has examined and compared them. He gathers up more and more leaves and moves in ever-widening circles while the philosopher and the princess smilingly regard his officious zeal. But no matter how many leaves he examines, it is to no avail – they are all dissimilar.

Conversation between philosophers

Consider then these shoes,
yellow boots with buttons, worn on the right,
more worn on the right than on the left,
consider for a hundredth time.

The lace-holes shinier than the leather,
a thin layer of dust, scuffed.

Consider them carefully, reflect upon them!

I see them, perfectly clearly,
the light is slanting, so it's afternoon,
so asymmetrically they're positioned,
as if to entice the eye to themselves!

I'm telling you, you do not see them,
there's someone standing in the way, he blocks your view.

But I see them, creased and wrinkled from wear.

You see a pair of shoes, yes, the light is slanting,
consider though *precisely these!* Say what you see!

It is impossible, there's someone standing in the way,
just there I can't see anything, just there.
Consider though instead *these* shoes,
yellow button boots, worn on the right...

It is impossible, there's something else that's in the way.

Then you've understood me!

Happiness

Someone in May woke at the sound of bells
and he recalled all the Sundays of his life,

went with cautious steps out into his garden
and found more birds there than ever before.

They sat in droves on the branches, in droves on the ground
but rose in a flutter of wings and flew off.

With calmer steps he walked into a remarkable day.

And in the innermost corner of the green bower
he refound happiness: the two marbles in the earth

that he as a two-year-old had hidden there and lost
and since had never managed to refind or to recall

till now, the moment that was opportune,
and that was happiness: they lay there clearly visible again,

and still untouched. How they gleamed in the warm light!

The conditions

There were two yellow houses that obscured the view.
But behind, glimpses of a road, green hillside,

distance, stillness so far that the air stood quivering.
And suddenly there were some people there, in red jerseys.

It passed so quickly that they were forgotten,
returned though as a fragment from a race

with end and start both hidden just as hopelessly from view.

Cyclists in an unclear section of the course, devoid of context,
so that the first could be the last or vice versa.

Only existing as long as not concealed from view.

Then there was a train that passed, with all its windows open
throughout the summer: a stronger memory, stronger time.

What an open landscape, roads, waving hands!

And when I looked up from my book the windows were all dark,
with curtains fluttering inwards from a voiceless gust of wind.

I looked and I looked. It could have lasted an eternity.
And understood that of such stuff all days are made.

The dog

'Home to a calmer country'
There is no calmer country than this one.

It was sunny and I was walking over the ice
the great expanses of ice the wind had swept clean,

and it was Sunday. Then I saw something strange,
a small black dog, completely alone,

running as fast as it could, straight as an arrow,
away from the land out towards the offing,

where all disappeared as mist on the horizon.
It ran very fast, without looking left or right,

and it was like a black ball of wool across the glittering blue
that the wind has caught and sweeps along with it.

I stood still for a long time gazing after it,
but it did not seem to stop and finally disappeared.

There is no calmer country than this one.

Picture

A gentleman by the name of Arenander is sitting at his table at night listening with half-closed eyes to the murmuring voices of inspiration. In front of the open window the curtain sways very faintly and slowly and the sheets of paper on the table with their varying degrees of whiteness flutter nervously. Faint sounds are also heard from a bumblebee confined in the darkness of the room.

A new scent comes through the window, completely cool. It is the arrival of a sudden rain, it lashes the ground, all becomes completely still. Dimly aware, Mr Arenander leans out and feels the change.

There is hunting in the air.

The bridges in Königsberg

In the city of Königsberg in Prussia
there is an island by the name of Kneiphoff
embraced by two arms of the River Pregel.
Seven bridges cross the two arms.

Seven bridges. And never more than once.
The water's heard now almost everywhere.
It is blind water, black water,
nocturnal water. Three kinds of water.

Churches and towers and sloping green roofs,
Here is a staircase. Here is a house.
Here is the dog that barks in the yard.
It is black, completely black. It barks.

Years. Years and days. As like each other as...
Do you hear me? I am shut in.
And no one hears. As Magdeburg hemispheres.
As unlike each other as: Apples.

From some fresh October; dog-barking,
voices, and only one bridge at a time,
never twice over the same bridge.
Some children always tread on each third stone,

and only each third one. The lure of the abyss.
The third door that always creaks.
Years. Years and days. Can you hear me? October,
and still no frost in the air.

So as to cross seven bridges in a row
and only cross each of them once,
one actually needs, says the mathematician Euler,
an eighth bridge. It does not exist.
Damned ice, that refuses to freeze!

A story from Russia

(metanovel)

There is a kind of largish building
where house and windows do not fit each other
and the result is an intolerable staring.
And then it is the windows that stare!

A rather thin man, on a visit to some chancery,
forgets a rough glove on a chair. He leaves.
It is found by Y. It is bitterly cold. He puts it on.
He is mistaken for Z. and meets with misfortune.

And we enter the primeval forests of European culture!
Tragedies, mistaken identities, elegant parties! And strictly speaking,
what strange pattern do these fates not form: M.A. ... alone,
'parmi les proses écrasées de sa jeunesse'.

But outside the prose writings it is completely still, winter night.
Examine the history closely and it could just as well not have existed,
the history: the princes, rebellions, stories. An obscurity.
Bitterly cold, the brightest moonlight and not even a sleigh track.

And then it is the windows that stare!

Snow

Early, in the light-grey darkness after snowfall
I heard the child speak, in word-strings and sounds.

It was a language from a foreign tongue,
one lighter and more gentle, it fell like snow.

In the faces of lovers for a helpless moment
one can see something before they know they are in love

and everything's restored. There is glass
and when it breaks one hears a special sound

and cracks through frozen lakes run on
so fast that no bird's flight can emulate it.

I do not know how many daybreaks I have seen
but none correctly matched the day that followed.

It passes. Does not linger. The crack runs on.

But in the light-grey, the indefinite, there we could reside.
You know what snow looks like once it has fallen.

Inscription on a stone

'I turn into stone and my pain remains.'
To translate. But into which language? And how?

I am asked to translate. It is asking to be translated,
as if it were not already written. Do other words exist?

Everything then is already written. And in the same characters.

The machines

Some of them came early, others late,
and outside the time where it exists
each and every one of them is homeless.

Heron's steam ball. The Voltaic pile. The ballista.
The great pit winder in Falun. Curiosities:
Den 'pneumatic winnower'
Una macchina per riscaldare i piedi

We only perceive machines as being homeless
when they belong to a different century.
And then they become distinct, acquire a *meaning*.

What do they mean? Nobody knows.

The flat-rod system: a device with two raising rods
that moving in reciprocal fashion
transfer power over large distances.
What does the flat-rod system mean?

DIE BERGWERKE IM HARZ ANNO 1723

The picture swarms with people. Human beings,
tiny as flies, are being hoisted and lowered in barrels
and the object marked 'j' in the picture, 'La Grande Machine',
at the fresh waterfall, drives all the cables.

No one has ever combined,
which would be perfectly possible,
a flat-rod system and a steam engine,
Hero's steam ball and the Voltaic pile.
The possibility still exists.

A foreign language that no one has spoken.

And strictly speaking:
Grammar itself is a machine
that among countless sequences
selects communication's strings of words:
the 'keen instruments', 'parts of childbirth',
the 'scream', the 'smothered whispers'.

When words have passed away, grammar remains,
and it is a machine. That means *what?*
Nobody knows. A foreign language.
A completely foreign language.
A completely foreign language.
A completely foreign language.

The picture swarms with people. Words,
tiny as flies, are being hoisted and lowered in barrels
and the object 'j' in the picture, 'La Grande Machine',
at the keen waterfall, drives all the cables.

Discussions

Older acoustic textbooks
advise us to perform strange experiments:

Visit an absolutely symmetrical garden
bounded on all sides by a wall
(with right angles)
visit the farthermost corner
and fire a pistol shot.

At a certain point the sound is inaudible.

Then you have found the acoustic node,
and it is invisible to the eye.

Let three persons form a group
at certain angles
round the completely smooth surface of a lake
and call out 'here' to each other in turns
and in a special rhythm.

No time passes before there are calls of 'here'
from all directions and unceasingly
and each person will no longer be able
to distinguish his own voice from the others'.

What a delightful antiphon!

A small electric clock
placed under the hermetic bell-jar
where the air is extracted by a suction pump
will finally indeed become quite inaudible.

In that way all suspicions are confirmed
about the defectiveness of the carrying agent,
its strange capacity to act of its own accord.

Of its own accord, of its own accord.

The time remaining is always extremely brief.
Sound is only produced by one who's very lonely.
The winter's very cold. All boats lie still in the ice.

And in clear weather the skates, the red sledges,
with a sound like that of a small bell,
under the 'hermetic bell-jar'.

Quiet, someone's speaking, is it you or me?

Echo, delightful nymph with the mutilated voice!

Draft of a fantastic zoology

(to Madeleine)

Certain species can harm each other
others can't, no matter how hard they try;
and there is a system in this, an order.

Certain poems do not want to stay put,
and have to be struck out word by word
till they're struck out back into the dark.
They come and turn so fast.
What do they want?
Observations. Reconnaissances.

Untouched night
and some insects flying
invisible: darkness in darkness
and something frighteningly soft against the cheek.
What is it that frightens?

The great pale-blue whales dance in the sea:
their nipples work under overpressure,
two and a half atmospheres.

Among the usual insects in the lamp
there are always some that seem *far too* agile
They are preparing ambushes.

Versuch einer Entwicklung der Fliege.

Everywhere the same, you lift up a stone,
and they move *far too* hurriedly.
Why such bad consciences?
Is it something they're preparing?

The species explain themselves,
but only to themselves.

'The strange thing is that I understand him,
know precisely how he felt,
– it frightens me that I understand.'

What is it that frightens?

I also suspect, for some time now,
that an *inner* zoology exists.
And it is superior!

'You have such a shifting gaze today!'

Bombus terrestris

When the air lies still, so do the lakes,
the great bright lakes, still like quicksilver.

Sleeping dogs' breathing grows ever more rapid.
The deepest sounds of all are felt as tremblings.

And held hidden in large organ pipes,
sixteen-footers and more, until it's time.

But out of small holes in the ground the sound emerges.

When air pressure falls, sounds of far trains get smothered,
they change and soundlessly move from track to track.

A flyer who lives in the depths of the forest
has folded his wings, and is asleep in the rain.

It is not at the start and not at the end.
It is mainland, vast tracts that are far

within maps and deep within time,
a forest of years protective on all sides,

and the larks soar up like a jubilant cloud,
but always some will fall dead, and perish.

Far too warm to freeze, far too cold
to reside, so far within the world

A backhanded winter, seasons inverted, a year that's reversed.
When the air lies still, so do the lakes.

But at the lowest height, a hand's breadth above the ground
the temperature changes distinctly: two degrees warmer

and some stifled brown sounds.
All natural science is a question of warmth

and obscuring low clouds.

C's monologue

'I' means 'the speaker'.
I Minotaurus. I Theseus.
I Daedalus. Etc.

This 'I' makes our drama a drama.

So swiftly the small shuttle darts
through the loom!

One person after another feels himself to be 'I'
– a completely differentiated feeling.
So skilfully is nature organised.

And not despair but tiredness,
the frightful fatigue
one feels in labyrinths
prevents me from saying much more.

Otherwise I would have spoken,
yes indeed,
I would have recounted.
You would have opened your eyes wide!

Or perhaps you would not have done so?

Or perhaps you are just as tired as I am?
(I have lately yawned quite openly
and only felt an immeasurable weariness
when anyone has censured me. For My Falseness.
My Coldness. My Tiredness. Etc.)

My tiredness causes me to see stones
small, small white stones at the bottom of a well.

Did you know that there are wells
just as deep as the towers of cathedrals?
Giddying spires and a cloud of birds,
jackdaws I think they are, around the tip?

Such images I even see in dreams.

I see images. And know that with just
some extremely small effort
there would... why don't more landslides occur?
Why can the stones lie still. When we cannot?

So swiftly the small shuttle darts!

I could recount. One drills wells,
100, 200 metres down into the ground
and it takes months and weeks.
I have seen someone working on such a well.
It was an unusually beautiful day, in autumn.
He lowered the explosives down the hole, a great deal,
lowered case-wise down to the bottom.
We waited for an eruption, a landslide
and that finally...

What do you think?

With a finger raised in the air
he drew our attention to the discreet knock
that was the explosion.

Notes from the 1860s

George Boole's book on the laws of thought appeared in 1854.
That is three years before Baudelaire's *Fleurs du Mal.*

In Boole lies the germ of the computers,
the ticking relays, the electronic valves, the future.

With charming indifference this algebra teaches us
that every class has something in common with 'the empty set.

The empty set. In a dream I meet Baudelaire,
small, transparent, with dark shadows under his eyes

and immediately ask for an opinion on Boole.
He regards this as a perfectly natural request

and begins with a quotation from Marquis de Sade:

'Nothing inspires us with such trembling and desire as knowledge
of the ticking relays, the electronic valve,

the distant roar from the hotter mines of the future'.

And breaks off, suddenly, as if he had said too much.

– *We're out on glassy ice, Sir! Do you realise that?*

– *Our age is the age when the wind is rising!*

The Wright brothers visit Kitty Hawk

In an agitated dream I saw it all explained:

Otto Lilienthal sails majestically in his glider
down the steep hill at Grosslichterfelde.

A strong wind was blowing, one for kites,
and someone spoke monotonously of 'the gnostic darkness'.

It was a warning, a whispering that came and went.

Bakunin boards the cargo ship *Andrew Steer*,
on a spring day, in Nikolaev harbour, among sheds and storehouses.

In the 19th century the sea often smells stale in periods of calm.
The revolutions are being prepared. The sea-fire sparkles.

And Milton Wright, Bishop of the Church of the United Brethren,
presents his sons Wilbur and Orville with one of Pénaud's models

not unlike a misshapen bird with a hungry neck.
Wind-tunnel experiments at the cycle factory wing

and the dry sand that whirls in stubborn wind.
What is good and bad about a kite? It flutters,

rises in a sudden rush but with a dead motion
at the instant it is about to snap the thread,

the all too short thread. In Africa the locomotives rust,
and the steamer Savannah with fluttering streamers

over a sea of unreal blue. Solemn columns of smoke.
Nature is always tangible: the aileron and the propeller.

Dresden. Hanoi. And 'the gnostic darkness'.

Elegy

The small tins that contain screws.
The small boxes with their well-worn trade marks,

originally intended to contain something else,
now contain screws. And nothing else.

A late-autumn day, in a strong wind magpies arrive
a whole dozen, flapping their wings at the roadside.

The philosopher Plato, aged like an elementary school teacher,
in an unwashed woollen sweater, observes them impassively

and knows that the archaic language they speak
is a dialect that now is unintelligible.

The world of ideas does not exist in rainy weather.

I too once had a form to see with
and then understood the visible world.

One of these tins, small tin-boxes, had a picture on it,
it was of a gold medal in Amsterdam.

It also contains screws. Nothing else but screws.

What birds do I know?
The wren. The wren steals soundlessly about.

At twilight between the hills and the houses.
Rests for a moment at the edge of a ditch.

Completely silent in flight.

The living and the dead

The ice-ferns on the window pane
The crystals that grow in caustic soda

'blindly' and in recognisable shapes.
Strindberg saw a draft of life

and the longing of dead things
to become living.

The cuddly animal that the child carries with it everywhere
and warms in its bed until it acquires a name

and the whole family talks about it
as one does about a real person.

The tin soldiers with their stiff unhappy faces.
The Moorish trumpeter who sits

high up in the wonderful organ in Oliva
and at a particular moment raises his trumpet

and blows to three points of the compass. He is Moorish.
All of that which imitates life, fails

and does not deceive us.

But hovering around these things, crystals,
toys, trumpeters

is an expression of sorrow, of melancholy.
And *that* is no imitation.

We sense it at once.
And are reminded of ourselves.

Regarding the deepest sounds

There is a stop on large organs,
a thirty-two-foot bass, contra-fagotto

a mighty quivering column of sound, late autumn
when the water in the wells rises

the underground network of watercourses and wells.
And it is more sorrow than sound.

At this lower boundary where music ends
something else wants to start,

more body than sound, body and darkness,
and late autumn when the wells rise,

but since it is below the ground,
below the music, below the lament

– it is unwilling to start, does not start
and thus does not exist.

Now it is closer, now it is distinct!
Now it's immediately heard in the entire area.

2

Till Eulenspiegel's merry pranks I

Our old friend Till Eulenspiegel
a central lyric poet advanced in years

and by mistake invited
to speak in Södertälje

to a circle of literary ladies
at a suburban library that owns thirty Widdings,

imagine that, thirty Widdings for twenty-nine ladies
explains why novels no longer exist:

(Heroes in novels would grow far too like each other
and no matter the circumstance incapable of action)

This had possibly been able to pass as 'brilliant'
if T. had not in the same breath made the mistake

of stating as if it were self-evident
that vaginal orgasm actually occurs

and that those evening newspapers
have little idea what they are talking about

(it is however becoming much less common, like songbirds)

Questioned by twenty-nine raging furies
about his vaginal experiences, T. replies

enigmatically

'This society's economists are also generally speaking
bad alchemists.'

Exit T. stage right.
And already less likely.

Till Eulenspiegel's merry pranks II

These intellectuals have started to become annoying,
extremely annoying

Is there anything more tiresome
than these dissembling play-actors

who stand on a stage and claim
to be proletarians.

There's only one thing that irritates me more:
These dissembling play-actors who

stand on a stage and profess

to be princes of Denmark

Darkness

Concerning my other side
my turned-away side
my uninhabited side:

Darkness in darkness
and deepest within the darkness
something to grapple with

strong enough to whirl me away like a leaf.

Concerning my relationship to music

I imagine a completely closed sphere.

This closed sphere contains something.

A strong magnetic field orders iron-filings into patterns.

Through compact walls.

That is how I use music,

and neither music nor I know
what we are actually dealing with.

Description of the Norberg quarry

The very black waters come very slowly
out of the forest and have an acrid taste

Gigantic black crayfish lurch uncertainly
over stones and stones, midway above the river

a starling hovers, and it is a thousand years
too early or a thousand years too late.

Black, inundated pits in distant hills
stretch farther down than the towers of churches

groping for something

Gigantic iron-encrusted wood decays
beneath verdure that is far too dense:

raspberries and snakes

The mattocks of medieval miners are still stuck in the trees

The whole region is waiting

Soon it will begin again

Warm and cold spaces

We go from warm spaces to cold
and from cold to warm spaces again.

The one being born screams suddenly at the light.
It knew all along the landslide was going to come.

How many mysterious places under the ground
are not built by what we call the heart!

Intercourse is more a way of remembering than forgetting.

At times we are dry snow crystals
swept by an ice-cold wind, swirling,

over expanses of gleaming ice. Without mercy.

On great hot summer days under mighty tree-tops
majestic stags graze in the deep-green shadow.

A mild breeze moves through the landscape.

I think there must also come an end to complaining.

Alba

In the sea-green bottle of the dream
live sleepers, both men and women

and over them the storm has no command

I recall a female body
of the dry, firm kind, a hot

uneasy body that refused to sleep
and asked me unintelligible questions.

A typhoon blew up in the early night
that heaved and howled in the shutters

the sea rose up and inundated many streets,
roof-tiles rampaged, flying through the air

and landing with a noise like thunder
in the surrounding precincts, a typhoon

that simply grew – I yearn back
to that night as if it were

a native land, my only native land
my home district, my lullabies, my house

and over them the storm has no command.

3

XI (Sestina)

There was a time each single frame was whole.
As is the tennis ball when hanging a
razor-sharp hundredth of a second, waiting
above the net. Not 'recently' or 'soon'
but a third something, which is all we see.
The rest is expectation or is time

that was, not mine though, someone else's time.
The clean shot is what once more makes you whole.
This is the sole reality we see.
Expectations and memories fill a
mainly random personality, soon
for the next ball you can see it waiting.

Who is it though that stands there ready waiting?
All time is eaten up by thoughts of time
that was, or something that will happen soon.
Expectations and the rest memories. Whole
is only he who no longer sees a
second ball in the ball there is to see.

Such an event as that we really see
is more anonymous than we were waiting
for. Years and princes existing in a
past age seem to live in a stiffened time.
By name we make the broken vessel whole.
It's borne with caution to a well that soon

seems deep and full of powerful voices. Soon
only a lonely echo's left – you see
the water's gleaming mirror, which is whole.
It lies down there below you waiting,
so inaccessible. It's you. Your time
is brief. A single stone's enough. And a

thousand splinters now glitter in a
well against whose grey-stone sides there soon
play flickering reflections. Which are time.
The only time we understand. We see
in splinters. In stiffened pose stand waiting.
The clean shot is what once more makes you whole.

We all live in a nameless world. We see.
We die as soon as we recall; die waiting.
There was a time each single frame was whole.

Sonnet XIV

Lonely shoal that the same uncertain wave
constantly washes with the same short beat.
Anxiously leaning buoy, the same gull's seat
day after day, beneath low skies that gave

off humidity and heat! And I gazed:
Eternity's long been in motion here,
I should have seen it, for the law is clear,
relentless, that applies – each wave thus phased

proves the same thesis, and I should recall
just how it was, though can recall no more,
which makes this gull so crucial. Its beak's caught

outlined against the waves. Scared its calm or
stubbornness might overcome me, both all
too great, across the waves my eyes still sought.

Sonnet XVII

Autumnal storm, warm wind. The moon obscured by trees.
A table, the boy just made out, dim from birth,
that scrapes the last drops from the bowl. This earth.
This warm wind. And now carried on this breeze

from a darkening lake a raw scent as of a
drowned man not recovered. And I, conferred
to be alive, walk through the grass. The self-same word
for that autumnal water scent, the moon that hovers

anxiously on watch, and then the night that goes
on growing, the yellow light that lights a small square
of a courtyard, moist earth that has a scent

of rotting pears, the cat up on its toes
that slyly sneaks through shrubbery. And there
came no rain. That word would have been heaven-sent.

Sonnet XXIV

I know something about you you don't know,
You are a dog. In frosty autumn earth
you're digging for a hidden bumblebee. A word
for this could be a 'truth affliction'. I know:

minus 'truth. Minus 'affliction. Secretly
we envy animals for this: there is no word
that captures what they do. Just as deferred
the outcome, wordless, with no uncertainty

through that thin body a fierce struggle streams.
You are a dog. The faint and stubborn sound
that leads you is an insect. And you don't know

that you will die. Outer events it seems
All coincide. The same faint stubborn sound.
You know something about me I don't know.

Sonnet XXVII

To one below the surface of the ice
the ice itself looks as if something white
and openings and wind wells where still quite
open water moves look, if there's a slice

of daylight left, as if expanses fraught
with darkness. And only he who knows aright
an exit lies in what is dark, that white
means darkness (that ice can so distort

conditions as they're pictured by the eye)
and who, against his instinct, swims away
from light towards the dark sees day again.

There is, once a small habit stirs, or by
a word that changes meaning, a chance, though stray,
of someone getting out. That he sees day again.

Sonnet XXVIII

It's late in coming. It had far to go.
There is no name for it but it's called grief.
A clenched fist is no more than a frail sheaf
of brittle fingerbones – it's hard to know

one's weakness properly. And very few
can view their weakness as a strong safe lair.
One stands on some huge Gustav Adolf square
and sees oneself forsaken. It's hard too

to cross a square like that. A hand that lies
open's nearly always empty. And a cage
where no bird's ever lived can easily

convey confusion. By what right do we
disdain a freedom that by nature, stage
by stage, would loosen cautiously all ties?

4

Ballad of the dogs

When Ibn Batutta, Arabian traveller, physician
and acute observer of the world,
born in Maghreb in the fourteenth century,
arrived at the city of Bulgar, he came to hear of the Dark.
The Dark was a land forty days' journey further north.
It was at the end of the month of Ramadan,
and when he broke his fast at sunset
he barely had time to pray his evening prayers
before day dawned once more. Birches stood white.
Ibn Batutta, Arabian traveller, never got further north
than to Bulgar. But the account
of the Dark and journeys to it fascinated him.
The journey is only undertaken by rich merchants.
They travel on hundreds of sledges
that are loaded with food and drink and firewood,
for up there the ground is covered with ice,
and no one can walk on it without slipping,
except the dogs, whose claws can gain a firm grip
in the eternal ice. Neither trees nor stones
let alone houses act as signposts on such a journey.
The guides in the Land of the Dark are the old dogs
that have made the trip many times before.
Such dogs command a price that can reach as high
as a thousand dinars, or more, for their knowledge
is indispensable. When one prepares a meal
the dogs are served before the human beings,
for otherwise the leader-dog will be enraged
and run off, leaving his master to his fate.
In the great Dark. After forty days' journey
the merchants stop in the Dark. They lay
their wares on the ground and return to their camp.
The following day they return and find
heaps of sable, ermine and miniver

a short distance from the piled-up wares.
If the merchant is satisfied with the barter he takes the furs.
If not, he leaves them there. Then those who live
in the Dark raise their bid by adding more furs,
or take back all that they had laid out
and ignore the stranger's wares.
That is their form of trading.
Ibn Batutta returned to Maghreb
and died at a ripe old age. But these dogs
that, mute and yet knowledgeable,
wordless and yet with blind assurance
trot across wind-whetted ice into the Dark
refuse to leave us in peace.
We speak, and the words know more than we do.

We think, and what we thought runs ahead of us,
as if what we thought knew something
we did not know. A message passes
through history, a code disguised as ideas,
but intended for others than us.
The history of ideas is not a psychological study.
And the dogs, with sure, swishing steps
ever deeper into the darkness.

Ballad on the paths in Västmanland

Beneath the visible writing of small roads,
gravelled roads, farm tracks, often with a comb
of grass in the middle between deep wheel ruts,
hidden beneath clear-felling's tangle of brushwood,
still legible in the dried-up moss,
there is another script: the old paths.
They go from lake to lake, from valley
to valley. At times they deepen,
become quite distinct, and large bridges
of medieval stone carry them over black streams,
at times they are lost over bare flat rocks,
one easily loses them in marshy ground, so
imperceptible that at one moment they are there,
the next not. There is a continuation,
there is always a continuation, as long as
one looks for it, these paths are persistent,
they know what they want and with their knowledge
they combine considerable cunning.
You walk eastwards, the compass persistently shows east,
the path faithfully follows the compass, like a straight line,
everything is in order, then the path swings northwards.
In the north lies nothing. What does the path want now?
Soon you come to a huge bog, and the path knew that.
It leads us around, with the reassurance of one
who has been this way before. It knows where the bog lies,
it knows where the rock face gets far too steep, it knows
what happens when it goes north instead of south
of the lake. It has done all of this
so many times previously. That is the whole point
of being a path. That it has been done
before. Who made the path? Charcoal burners, fishermen,
women with skinny arms collecting firewood?
Outlaws, timid and grey as the moss,

still in their dream with the fratricide blood
on their hands. Autumnal hunters in the wake
of trusty foxhounds with their frost-clear bark?
All and none of them. We make it together,
you too make it on a windy day when
it is early or late on the earth:
We write the paths, and the paths remain,
and the paths are wiser than we are,
and know all we wanted to know.

Elegy for a dead labrador

There can occur here, in the midst of summer,
some days when suddenly it is autumn.
The blackbirds in the trees assume a shriller tone.
The stones stand very emphatic out in the water.
They know something. They have always known it.
We know it too, and do not like it.
On the way home, in the boat, on just such evenings,
you could stand stock-still in the bow, composed,
and sniff the bearings of scents coming over the water.
You read the evening, the faint streak of smoke
from a garden, a pancake being made
three kilometres away, a badger
that in the same twilight was standing somewhere
snuffing in the same way. Our friendship
was naturally a compromise; we lived
together in two different worlds: mine,
mostly letters, a text that passes through life,
yours mostly scents. You had talents
I would have sacrificed a great deal to possess:
the ability to let a feeling, eagerness, hate or love,
surge like a wave through your entire body,
from nose to tip of tail, the inability
ever to accept that the moon is a fact.
At a full moon you always complained out loud against it.
You were a better gnostic than I am. And consequently
constantly lived in paradise.
You had a habit of catching butterflies, in mid-leap,
and munching them, that some people found repulsive.
I always liked it. Why
couldn't I learn from you? And doors!
In front of closed doors you would lie down and sleep,
sure that sooner or later the person must come
who would open the door. You were right.

I was wrong. I ask myself now, now that this
long speechless friendship is over for good,
if there was possibly anything I was able to do
that impressed you. Your firm conviction
that I was the one who brought about thunderstorms
doesn't count. That was a mistake. I think
that my unshakable belief that the ball existed
even when it lay hidden behind the sofa
gave you some sort of an inkling of my world.
In my world most things existed concealed behind
something else. I used to call you 'dog'.
I wonder a great deal if you perceived me
as a larger, more boisterous 'dog',
or as something else, for ever unknown,
that is what it is, exists in the property
in which it exists, a whistle
through the night-time park that one has got used to
returning to without really knowing
what it is one is returning to. About you,
and who you were, I knew nothing more.
One could say, from this more objective
point of view: We were two organisms. Two
of these loci where the universe ties a knot
in itself, short-lived, complex structures
of proteins that had to become increasingly
complicated in order to survive, until everything
bursts and becomes simple again, the knot
untied, the mystery gone. You were a question
simply directed towards another question,
and neither had the other's answer.

Song of the world's depths, the eye's depths, life's brevity

The moral law within us. The starry heavens above us.
But there exists starry heavens below us also.
Galaxy under galaxy ever deeper in an endless well
that our still medieval world picture forgets.
It still connects *heaven* with *upwards*,
fails to understand that if there are stars above us
there are also stars below us. That
glimmer in the dark. The moral law also must exist
below us as well as above us, a law for those
who endlessly fall, angels plunging in the
comet tails of their long hair, collapsing suns,
astronauts asleep on board their spaceships,
the Christians on board their cathedrals, asleep
in their sepulchres, huge coffins of marble
and black basalt, and all on its way through the
maelstroms of the deep, towards resurrection's shore,
which through endless topographical *involutions*,
endless mapping of the set *into* itself,
is precisely the shore we have never left.
Here all of us sit, invisible, knights with greaves
and astronauts in protective helmets and
Heraclitus, the little bent old man at his acrid fire
of hard olive-wood, all sit at the same shore
watch the bleak at play, sense the faintly acrid smell
of sunken logs of timber, see smoke from a laundry house
stretched out by the first autumn wind across the lake.
How fast must the falling angels fall
to keep pace with us on our shore?
Do they glow with the heat of falling? Or with the force
that propels them? And is this moral law for
the endlessly falling, for the unfathomable depths
and their more or less voluntary travellers

on a par with the law for the eternally rising?
Indeed, much is obscured in the far too dense
willow avenues of East Prussia, far too shallow
is many a marl-pit: there is a duty,
certainly, but its negation exists as well.
How right to forgo ego and speech! How
right to create an ego for oneself where there was none,
how right to assert oneself, how right to harbour desire!
Philosophers love to determine how the crofters,
day-labourers, the individual soldiers, the magnificently
liveried servants up at the back of light carriages
are to have things, and most of all, I would point out,
what they are to be able to wish for themselves:
everything from the duty to plough for free
to the geraniums in the window which we,
that is to say the crofters, are to enjoy
with a dispassionate gaze. Exit Immanuel.
Abysmal snowstorm of galaxies below us,
insatiable desire within us, for all that can be desired,
to all that this darkness, which is that
of the other person, can offer in the way of lust,
secret knowledge, seduction, hatred.
Oh Sister Messalina! There is a needle-point!
And on this needle-point we live, like the angels!
(Perhaps we even are angels, Sister Messalina?)
The great, secretive suns live and die
are lit and extinguished in their mysterious depths,
as long as the Well suffices, and the dark
masses of the gravitational collapses cave
powerfully in on themselves at the boundary where
time's slender thread is stretched out and becomes a
vast landscape, where space is contracted
to a needle-point. There we live in
eternity, oh Sister, under this Second Law,
a law for those that endlessly fall, gleaming,
and fill for ever this darkness with their glow.

Oh Heraclitus, how short the November day is,
it grows dark over the lake, Your fire starts
to stand out more strongly in the dark, You yourself
disappear among flickering shadows. With ancient
signs the familiar constellations appear
in the sky, November's wind moves among the reeds'
brittle stems, which move with an
ever drier sound. And across the western sky
the track of a falling angel like some script.
Oh Master Heraclitus, it is time for us,
over the fire, to warm a tankard!

5

The silence of the world before Bach

There must have existed a world before
the Trio Sonata in D, a world before the A minor Partita,
but what was that world like?
A Europe of large unresonating spaces
everywhere unknowing instruments,
where *Musikalisches Opfer* and *Wohltemperiertes Klavier*
had never passed over a keyboard.
Lonely remote churches
where the soprano voice of the Easter Passion
had never in helpless love twined itself round
the gentler movements of the flute,
gentle expanses of landscape
where only old woodcutters are heard with their axes
the healthy sound of strong dogs in winter
and – like a bell – skates biting into glassy ice;
the swallows swirling in the summer air
the shell that the child listens to
and nowhere Bach nowhere Bach
skating silence of the world before Bach

The didapper

(strictly: Great Crested Grebe)

In the pure clear autumn evenings
in small groups ahead of the motorboat's prow.
And disappearing without fear, without flurry,
simply because
disappearing is its natural art-form.

I have often wished
that I could follow it
also on its other flight.
Does it view the water's surface
as a second sky?
What are its heavy wing-strokes under water like?

Does it consider itself
the same bird in two separate spaces?
The one ruled by winds,
the other by cool deep currents?

The tree with quivering leaves.
The long tresses of the sea-grass in the current
where the cold bottom spring meets the lake.

How can it fuse
such separate things into one life?
Or does it consider itself
two birds
that meet for an instant at the

dizzying, mute boundary of the water's surface?

Poems from Africa 4

The smell from an old wooden cupboard,
Hôtel Résidence, Saint-Louis:
Scent of malaria a century old,
moss that's dried, camphor:
neither moss nor camphor,
and the sea close, with heavy breakers.
Something that is bitter acrid and sweet,
and has been shut in a long time:
Here the river begins.
Here Tekrour, the river kingdom, once began.
Here Borom N'Dar once ruled.
'The Ruler of N'Dar'.
Here the moon rises silver-white
out of the sea's red mist.

6

The eel and the well

In old Scania there was a custom:
young eels from the sea were let down
into the black depths of the wells.
These eels then spent their entire lives
imprisoned in the darkness of the deep wells.
They keep the water crystal-clear and clean.
When on occasions the well-eel comes up,
white, frighteningly large, caught in the pail,
blind and coiling in and out
of its body's enigmas, unaware,
everyone hurries to submerge it again.
I often feel myself as being
not only in the well-eel's stead
but well and eel at the same time.
Imprisoned in myself, but this self
already something else. I exist there.
And wash it clean with my twisting,
miry, white-bellied presence in the darkness.

Concerning everything that still hovers

As yet my grave is nowhere visible.
And thus I too am hovering:
resting, myself, unknowing,
I too in a sea of air, an atmosphere.
Floating with the floating,
living with the living,
resting with the resting,
and, perhaps also, without knowing it,
dead with the dead.
There is no word for this:
it is a way of hovering.
'In the Sea of Air' like the aeronauts of old,
and you are this sea yourself.
Once, in Texas, at six o'clock in the morning,
swimming across the crystal-clear water
of a very deep swimming pool
actually meant for high-divers,
swimming to me suddenly turned to flying.
Gazing down through the goggles' small windows
to the well-cleaned black and white squares below,
from exactly the height where one no longer survives
in a free fall, I could for an instant vaguely sense:
To constantly be falling, be in one's fall
and yet to fly, borne by something invisible.
We see through and smile at the old painters
and their childish trick
of placing some birds deep in the picture,
very small, floating like meaningless signs
between earth and air, between light and dark,
between water and land, in short,
the kind of things that exist between the differences,
the twilight things that create the depth
which linear perspective on its own cannot achieve.

So do all mortals float within
their own picture, somewhere in the twilight,
and for this floating there is no name.

So too do signs float over the white sheets of paper,
the rooks over the snow, the good over evil time.
So does everything float. It *stands* like the angels stand,
in unprecedented motion.
And for the world's flight there is no name.

Placenta

This formless, lobated organ
that is expelled after birth.
Neither mother nor child, neutral,
in the same way the innermost void
within true insomnia
is a completely neutral place.

There always exists something
that is between usual states,
neither the one nor the other.
Towards this Between
I feel a wry friendship,
a kinship even.

It has the real world's
large vacant, candid face.

Winter in a Westphalian village

Someone has placed a bowl of fine porcelain
over the ponds and hills and trees.

At times this bowl is lit up from above
and something stands out. Only vaguely.

The water of the ponds is not exactly frozen.
but not exactly water either.

A state between states, where light
from a distant car in the dusk

vibrates, like light from the depths of space.
Far too ancient to maintain its wavelength.

At a bend in the road, a faint warming smell of pigsties.
Two wild duck fly up, purposefully,

as if the underworld were full of birds.

(Wellensich 1981)

Old master

The last few days
this summer has been an old master.

Will he be able to pull himself together
and manage it one last time?

And in early September it happens:
the sky clears, the rowan bushes are on fire,

it becomes warm one final time
and the sound of bumblebees grows, drones as in May.

And yet it's even so not quite the same.
The blue is just a shade too blue

when the wind ruffles the water,
the tree-tops are too vibrantly ablaze.

A rhetoric is lurking here.

Austin, Texas

A small peaceful place where I could just do
my own thing, and without reproaches.

I was in search of something like that
ever since my first day in primary school.

But it wasn't of course easy to know
that such a place actually existed.

And strictly speaking every country
I've lived in was a foreign country.

How strange, not to say unusual:
This *staying* and *remaining*.

The first time was a spring night in 1972.
The whole world was a dark, hot, humid

incomprehensibility from the plane ramp onwards.
Groped for a window. But was already outdoors.

I put up at Villa Capri,
a motel that disappeared many years ago,

Weinstock and Rovinsky fetched me
in the thundering, warm rain, both in string vests

and the lightning flashes photographed their still young
energetic faces with black beards.

And strongest, the smell of rotting wood,
vegetation, mud and southern honeysuckle.

I forgot my poplin coat at the hotel.
Precisely as Dr Freud would have it!

But in the humidity there was music! It streamed out of all
the streets! Ballads and blues and a special kind of

pensive jazz. It resembled nothing I had heard before.
It came from a warmer air and scented soil.

Everyday, all of this, for a decade.
The large serious faces of the students,

grocery bills and the dog that digs
far too much in the rose-bed.

To Benjamin everything is self-evident.
And yet never completely so to me.

Never more to really need the woollen mittens
that sleep like kind kittens in the wardrobe!

A place where everything grows, just as long as
you let it fall into the earth. Under large trees

that are glad of any wind that comes.
Certain things always remain incomprehensible:

the storm of insect noises in the hot night,
the mysterious warm darkness. A lone trumpet

blue as the night from a lit-up window.
Sunrises when the whole world is ablaze

and the black herons perch heavy
as Huginn and Muninn in the old dead river-trees.

Rovinsky no longer lives here, and Weinstock's
hair and beard are white. Telephones ring,

and want to sell credit cards. Office blocks spring up
and have glass facades as black as the river.

But the shadow under the trees is what it is and in
the river under the bridge huge carp are sleeping.

They will always be there, no boy will catch them.

Elegy on the old Mexican woman and her dead child

Am I mistaken –
or is the air thinner here?

Could also here, in *this location*,
a swallow gain a winghold?

Already in the bathroom mirror
the eccentric old man

in the process of slowly freeing itself
from my face, vaguely appears:

resilient, sun-burnt, wrinkled,
with ever colder blue eyes,

the last of the men I shall be.
Not yet complete, although already intimated.

I try to recall the face that once
was here in the mirror:

blond, round-cheeked, content,
supported on its chubby elbows.

How can we, so many men, inhabit
the self-same body?

An old woman in Mexico, the newspaper relates,
was admitted to hospital for a stomach complaint.

The examination that showed the eighty-six-year-old
had carried an embryo for more than sixty years.

A stone-child, *lithopedion*, that weighed nine hundred grams,
had followed her throughout her life.

She was both mother, one could say, and grave
for one and the self-same child.

Graves, these cavities, urns, vaults,
marble crypts or simple hollows in the ground,

which for millennia we have insisted on,
are naturally *mothers*, each and every one:

helplessly we still seek to reunite
the dead one with the starting point.

The Mexican woman, in her way,
was *the ideal grave*. And that of her child

a model life? Mocking bird, what's your errand?
You have so many voices, and I do not know

which of them should be taken seriously.
A times the mocking, the lamenting sometimes,

and there is a kind of gulping sound at times
on certain days in early spring

when moisture clings still to the oak-tree's moss
as if you really did not get it said somehow.

Mocking bird! What secret are you, sitting in
the green oak-tree, trying to swallow?

I too am an old Mexican woman,
I too bear a dead child within me,

though my child's odd for it can speak,
in actual fact it talks unceasingly,

prattles and babbles as does every child
that has not learnt to speak; it's hard to tell

just what it wants, though that it wants is clear.
I'm not intractable, quite the reverse,

I feel I stand *in loco patris* and really try
to understand just what this child

wants from its life, which is its death.
But it's not easy. It's so unlike me.

And it knows nothing of this world.

Elegy for the outer boulevards

Théâtre Récamier, October evening 1971, and outside
the first real downpour of rain that year was falling,

a girl passed quickly across the courtyard with a cheese
(it was immensely important it did not get wet)

all traffic stood still for a moment,

really still, right from the outer boulevards
and right into the city's heart. And this heart beat.

How brief are the moment of the open window
and the mighty sound of rain! So much could have

been said then, in the heart's instant! How many cities
of a strange kind does the heart not build underground

cities that are never inhabited? Or
are they even so inhabited? In secret?

What do we know about those gliding by, the teeming,
the silent ones swiftly gliding over the soul's walls

as shadows come and go
over the dark beds of streams? What do we know

of the possible ones and their teeming? We walk through
the outer boulevards and know nothing about the centre.

More and more often it seems October to me and
I would gladly, tiny as a comma, live

among my own letters in such a forest.
And with no other sound. Than the sighing of the wind.

And at the easel, in the mild storms of glazes,
when two colours quietly and solemnly

cross over into each other, something that's indisputably me
and could not be anyone else. It is the boundary;

it is neither the one colour nor the other.
It is neither air nor light. And is not 'me'.

It is simply this: they move across and never stay just in the one.
And the sighing of the wind. That is always there.

(to Dr Margareth Wijk, Lund)

Elegy for lost and forgotten objects

The winter gloves that ended up at the bottom of the drawer.
The old brass trolling-spoon under a torrent of screws.

And a hammer, with mortar on the shaft,
that must have been in the family since '39

and that suddenly the earth has swallowed up.
All those things that were once so close to us

must now remember for themselves what drawer they belong to.

They can't rely on me any longer. And are on their own.

I remember what they looked like, how they felt in my hand,
even remember the hammer on a summer's day

in the distant forties when I was
much too small to be able to lift it properly,

and how my father carefully took it away from me.

The world, a labyrinth for lost

and forgotten objects, from the old swords
in the never-opened bronze-age burial sites

to the reading glasses that got lost the day before yesterday,
has them all in mind. No cause for alarm.

And you who go around searching so eagerly?
Are not you yourself such an object of searching?

And something tells you, one evening when something was refound,
scratched and rusty but still the same as ever

in the drawer under the torrent of bolts and locks
that all this hunting for things

only mirrored your own fervent wish:
that someone should be hunting you with the same zeal.

Carl Fredrik Hill visits Lake Buchanan

'The new school,' Carl Fredrik Hill writes
in a letter, from Montigny to Lund, in June 1876,

'involves carrying out one part only of the picture
and blurring all the rest.' Now it is June 1989,

and today nature is painting precisely so,
it too a stubborn master soon to be confused.

A lone pelican goes at the water's edge beneath a
tropical-grey sky. So heavily its wings beat!

This mournful inland lake has now put on its
July colour – a molten silver in a silver mist.

Alchemy. In the hermetic vessel now and for so long
the elements' transformations are taking place.

Yes, silver over the hot dead calm.
To swim round the boat is like swimming in tea-water.

It is not anchored. It is far too still.
Nor anchor line would be sufficient anyway.

It's several hundred metres here. We too,
the swimmers, are birds. And do not notice it.

Far off the sound of a speeding boat.
Moving in another direction. In silver. Believe me

there are places, in both geography and dreams,
that could not be painted in any other way.

So does form emerge out of the formless,
and the formless out of form.

Maestro Hill! How much you knew after all!
And how self-evident wasn't it

that you afterwards had to place in forgetfulness!
Let it fall deep into its forgetful waters.

The coin that seesaws down into the depths and is gone.
'The score or so pictures which he did himself

that were in the room he apparently never paid
the slightest attention to afterwards.'

(to Dr Birgit Rausing)

7

Sörby elegy

Wild chervil and chamomile surge against the
slag foundations of foundries that once were there.

The swallows weave an invisible web, and inside,
in a paler light and with the scent of ageing wood,

here the summer grows still. Mild and patient,
as if only with difficulty they recall their places,

things from vanishing years hang and stand.
A fyke with an ring of silvery juniper that has

not caught a pike since the end of World War I.
A pike spoon made by Bricklayer Ramsberg,

a quiet man who had lost a thumb.
A small boat that was once owned by a child

put together of far too coarse blocks.
A peeling garden table that was owned

by a grandma who lived to be a hundred.
And the shadow beneath her raspberry bushes

passes for a moment, like a cloud,
a very small cloud in some other sky.

The grandfather's hammer with its shiny haft.
Huge shears from a sheet-metal workshop in Nibble.

I am probably the last person who can remember
where they came from, from Platelayer Claeson in Nibble,

and after me they are free, as free as an arrow-head
that someone finds amongst the gravel of a river bed.

We give back, but only hesitatingly and meagrely.
How absent-minded and mild things become

when they are once more let loose, finally,
and gain their long holiday vacation, from the human

domain, from intentions and actions and words.
How are they to recall their places in tables and drawers?

In wasp buzzing and tar smell, in the darkness of the shed
it hangs, lies and stands: so many an abandoned thing

from some other year. And the June wind veers.

When did people's mouths get wet?

The small boy asks: Lars,
when did people's mouths get wet?

What? Well I think
they were wet from the start.

They're certainly wet in the womb.
There it's always wet anyway.

Certain things make them wetter,
that's for sure.

Yes, people's mouths have always been wet.

Being wet comes to an end.
But there's no particular day it starts.

Zones

There are of course dead places in the mind,
zones we evacuated so early on

that we do not know they ever existed.
What were they like, what would have grown there?

They can start behind the forest edge ahead.
And we do not go there.

Only when at times
on our way through the labyrinthine landscape

we feel a special type of grey emptiness
(nothing else not anger not grief)

search for a while through the tracts
where we long since are dead.

Come tired body

Come tired body, come tired mind
It's all the same though you we fail to find

Our path's lit by the lantern's glare
it flickers though. Perhaps a house was there

but maybe we passed by it on our way
and never saw it on that plot of ground

The sure path's one we will not find some day
The sure path's one that someone else once found.

If the mind exists,
it is of no importance
if it is mortal or immortal.

The important thing's the mind exists.
(For bodies all look so alike.)

Basilides' syllogism

God created the world out of nothing.
(The Book *Vereyshit*)

Out of nothing comes nothing.
(*The Philosopher*)

Ergo:
This world is created,
but is under the dominion of the void.

Clocks

Clocks tick hesitantly in tropical spaces.
Time takes the children along and makes them big.

Where the children were is suddenly only silence.

Dry flies, almost weightless on the calm
black surface.

And the capacity to express precisely this.

Audience with the Muse

I dreamt that I visited a country
that was so young that it had not yet
decided on its name and its flag.
It felt incredibly strange;
in a sense one didn't know where one was.
An unknown dark-haired lady
extremely expensively dressed, but tastefully,
sat down at my table.
It turned out she was the Muse of Poetry.
So courteous, so unassuming in everyday life,
I thought.
Something of the perfect female tourist hostess.
        One couldn't imagine that so important a person
or rather personification
        could be so unpretentious and generally amiable.

I was promised that the Republic
        would soon acquire a name,
and a flag.

I answered:
        absolutely no need to take any extra trouble on my behalf...

The card

This card does not entitle the owner
to a seat in first class.

This card does not entitle the owner
to a seat.

This card does not entitle the owner
to the Order of Charles XIII,

in the blue ribbon of the Order of the Seraphim

This card does not entitle the owner
to sexual services, provisions

or a roof over his head.

This card does not entitle the owner
to own other cards.

This card does, however, entitle the owner
to, as long as he wishes, own his card.

Berth

Suddenly I was in Sweden again.
Public authority phoned, offered me a berth
paid for by the Municipality.

Excellent. Will come and look.

Turns out a thirty metre long
roughly three metre wide channel has been dug up
in the middle of the Wallin cemetery.

Here a boat will lie fine.

But how on earth have you envisaged
getting it out onto open water?

It isn't to come out.
Your boat is to lie here.

Aristotle and the crayfish

We went to buy angling-worms
in a shop clearly intended for this purpose.

And we found what we were looking for;
fat, squirming angling-worms,

a kind the fish here seem to prefer.
But in the middle of this room a large old-fashioned earthenware jar

blue, round and full of young crayfish.
And my young son was inconsolable

at having to leave these wonderful creatures.
We bought two, and released them

in our clean, glass-clear aquarium,
where the goldfish moved slowly and solemnly

like old poets in a distinguished academy. And behold,
a great darkness descended upon all things:

here expressions of opinion and discussions took place
beyond our comprehension; only seaweed

that floated up to the surface bore witness to
the contention that here was secretly taking place.

On the third day the aquarium cleared once more.
And became as before. But no crayfish

were visible. We decided they now
were living like hermits, in greater wisdom,

a life withdrawn from public life
down below the sand beds.

So it continued for a long time, until one day
I opened my Aristotle

and found a very small crayfish corpse
flat as a plant in a herbarium

precisely in the short section where the Philosopher
talks about memory and recollecting

the past. And this chapter
one of the best things

ever written about memory,
will now for ever be associated

with an odour not easy to forget,
one of a slightly rotten crayfish.

Variations on a theme by Silfverstolpe

11
(Villanelle I)

The body remembers. Images were all the soul could see.
The desires of the flesh, the sharp pain of a nail.
What's cold and white-hot no soul keeps eternally.

Even types of pain can't be exchanged. A grazed knee
and the wasp in the grass. Likenesses will always fail.
The body remembers. Images were all the soul could see.

Each hour had something sharp and something soft that only
it was made for. Each love's scent is unique in type and scale.
What's cold and white-hot no soul keeps eternally.

Once we drank tea at this table, now all one can see
are mouldered bits of teak to tell the tale.
The body remembers. Images were all the soul could see.

Of these once warm days rotten bits of teak are all you see.
Predicting logic for desire and pain's to no avail.
What's cold and white-hot no soul keeps eternally.

Above a trackless forest hosts of birds cry noisily.
Just birdsong did the body know, and without fail.
The body remembers. Images were all the soul could see.
What's far too cold and white-hot no soul keeps eternally.

16

(Villanelle II: An old barometer)

Just what it measures nobody now knows.
The column of mercury stands resolutely still.
Who cares if an old barometer still goes?

An engraved plate lists the weather's tos-and-fros.
From *'Very Dry'* to what your fancy will.
Just what it measures nobody now knows.

Seven modalities the inventing optician chose.
The empty places other words could fill.
Who cares if an old barometer still goes?

The stave of mercury is broken into rows
that are air-bubbles, time-scraps, overspill.
Just what it measures nobody now knows.

What atmospheric quirks need one suppose?
Would *Earthquake* some new life perhaps instil?
Who cares if an old barometer still goes?

In instruments like this secrets repose,
some moment measured right when all stands still
Just *what* it measures nobody now knows.
Who cares if an old barometer still goes?

8

The small roads

The salesman on the blue bike
had a professional pride.
He knew the landscape,
even the smallest roads.
Those that went down to the canal
and where the wind in the aspen trees
blurred with the sound of water,
almost soundless at first for several kilometres
and then powerful and audible
where the sluice gates were open
along high avenues
of pines that were frighteningly tall
that stood there like dark churches
and he showed the boy the way into them.
He knew where the wild strawberries were
but also the angry dogs
that could run through a whole village.
And he showed the boy everything.
And the boy learned it all.
Without knowing what he actually learned.

All crazy small objects

All these strange
small objects
that come to us in the course of our lives
each one from its own location
each one from its Logos.

The old pruning knife
with its worn wooden haft
and its blade worn thin
found on a pavement in Arles.
And the sculpture
of brass turned green
that an artist once
welded for me out of old door handles
in a studio close to what was once the Berlin Wall
in Marie Luisenstadt.

That artist was completely crazy
and could only be addressed
in *the schizophrenic language*.
His work resembles, if anything at all,
a spider. But without a web.

A small azure bottle
with a fish's mouth up at the cork
from some rubbish dump.
A child once gave it to me.

They do not speak of course.
And neither are they 'symbols'
of something or other.

They have come down
from the firmament of forms
to stay
for a short while
on writing desks
and in window recesses

And one is grateful for their visit.

How the winters once were

That cold green streak
that was morning
had nothing in common
with us.

And the proud plumes of chimney smoke
rose straight up.
To some god who liked
such vertical movements.

And the scrunching underfoot!
Oh that indescribable scrunching:

no one could approach unheard
that was for sure.

And the suspicion that life
perhaps really *was* meaningless

and not just in Schopenhauer
and the other daring old guys.

But here too
under the sky's white plumes of smoke.

In-between days

In those white, strangely meaningless
days between Christmas and New Year

when the snow was still at its thinnest
and the skating marsh only just frozen

one always had to visit Hallstahammar
where the entire family lived

The yellow bus took us from Munkgatan
and over the only tolerably white fields

with murders of crows that swirled up
towards an early blue-green twilight

It was like coming to an older world

Grandma Tekla, white-haired with *The Book of Revelation*
in hands like old tree-roots

Old people with kick-sleds
made their way along the factory's main street

leaning into a wind that was not there
The low rows that housed Claesson's metal shops

were still there beneath unkempt apple trees
And everything was a sullen, sulky Old Sweden

with meeting house, rolling-mill, waterfall
And the smell of the last apple

that was still left in winter's brittle grass
That was left 'forever' there.

Fichte by the kerosene lamp

When the soft darkness of August
suddenly closed in
it was as if the lake down there
quickened its pulse, breathed otherwise
unknown animals perhaps peered out of
their holes in the bank.
And the kerosene lamp was lit.
It was like a small lighthouse
in various ledges of glass and porcelain
and the hot stream of heated air
must be kept away from the curtain.
Very careful about that,
never place the lamp under the curtain.
It produced, strictly speaking, a great deal of heat
(the difference could clearly be felt in the room)
and not much light. And around this lamp flew
an angry small steel-blue insect
the philosopher Fichte had somehow
extracted himself from the thick brown book
on the table,
where he presumably lived.
Circled until the flame took him.
But then the evening was over.

Aunt Svea

She lived for eighty-six years.
Strictly speaking not that long.
(Seen from a broader perspective.)
In the winter of 1919 she was a little Småland girl
who was really pleased with her new shoes.
(She had never had any new shoes before.)
Until she dried them
over the red-hot stove in school
and discovered that the soles
were made of cardboard.

She went home through swirling new snow
in her stockinged feet
– I have been told.

And lived on, hardworking and bitter,
for eighty years
ending up sitting lonely and childless
in her dark kitchen.

A men's choir

The voice one has when
talking to small children
and large dogs
is not the same
as that at the hairdresser's
or from the lectern.
It comes from another life
from far, far away
one that maybe never existed

whereas the voice
one has
when caressing a woman's breast
or belly
is a third voice
that comes from a third world
(green warm moist shadow under
huge ferns, marshland and
huge birds that fly up).
And there are many, many more.

Not my own voice –
and not exactly that of anyone else.
Is there such a thing as
The voices in between?
I recall your foot
still warm with morning.
I imagine
it must be like that.
And if one could hear
all the voices at the same time
one would get the impression

of a men's choir
defiantly executing
a breakneck series of assonances.

The tired

The tired old boats
break their moorings in the first autumn gale
and go adrift,
heavy, half water-logged,
melancholy
and quietly philosophical
until they start to rot away in the reeds

Of course Superman is Clark Kent

(in memory of W.V.O. Quine, Harvard, who passed away
on Christmas Day 2000)

To Bertrand Russell and quite a while after
this thing about *existence* was not so complicated.
Existence was a crow
that came flying when one needed it,
a reversed E
which said that something
that called itself 'x' was a value
of a variable. Which was often called 'f'.
$\exists x$ (fx): there is an x which is f
$- \exists x$ (fx): it is not the case that there is an x which is f.
Using this method one could demonstrate that
it is not the case that someone is now King of France
and bald.
So this assertion does not become meaningless
but false.

Using this method it is easy to prove
both that Mr Pickwick is a girl
(because it is not the case that he is a man)
and
that Clark Kent is not Superman.

'To be is to be a value on a variable,'
said the great Quine who always
greeted me so kindly at the tobacconist's
on Harvard Square.

Did we really *believe* all this
in my youth?
Or did we just pretend?
So what are we to do with Clark Kent?

Surely everybody knows that
Clark Kent is Superman?
Not to mention
the poor *Universe*
that goes around alone
looking in vain for
its variable to be a value on.

Exit Dr Quine,
and flights of angels sing thee to thy rest.

But back to our question:

What does all this about existing mean?

Tennis balls return
but not yesterday's tennis ball
only *this one*.
For there is only one tennis ball,
precisely *this one*,
and there has never been another one.

I biked along the river Isis, walled in
by greenery, past all the locks,
one early summer evening in '57
with the Danish philosopher Søren Nordentoft
who wanted to maintain that for Heidegger
existence is something completely different than for Russell.
The dark-brown cello note
that like a distant dynamo
hums behind our lives?
Or something else:
there exists *a single* tennis ball
that can be returned.
And there was never any more
but only this.

It was difficult to forget the picture of Heidegger
in his Rector's black uniform in Freiburg,
but what he had to say about Being,
or as it rather should be referred to, *Dasein*
right here and now and never anywhere else
was undeniably a bit more like Life
than this teeny-weeny reversed E.
Dasein can never be a reversed E.
It is hereness, presence, pain and compulsion.
This secret thing that holds things upright.

'And quite honestly,' the old logician added,
while he discreetly brushed the chalk dust
from shy and slender hands that
suggested they had never caressed a woman,
at the end of a long, sweaty demonstration,

'quite honestly
I have never really understood
just why *existence* is to be considered so important.
Unicorns, imaginary numbers still do all right,
and Mr Pickwick and all his friends.
Not to mention God.
Of course Superman is Clark Kent.

And we can take the rest when meeting next.'

Highly delayed, polemical attack on a Greek patriarch totally unprepared for such an eventuality

The patriarch Athanasius was accused
during his lively life

of both this and that.
The Arians had it in for him.

Among these accusations
there is also one of smuggling grain.

One thing and the other
can probably be dismissed

as frivolous arguments at a time
when arguments could be worse.

But this thing about grain smuggling!
Doesn't it sound like a completely

authentic story? Why should
a Greek patriarch engage in

such a strenuous and cumbersome
activity if not for profit?

And who would come up with such an
uninteresting form of crime for him

when heresy, sodomy, inflammatory speeches
against Caesar Alexander, and his court,

offer so much more worthy alternatives?
I do not know if it is all that important,

or if it is that sort of argument
that can be used somewhere else

than in precisely this poem
and even there quite by chance:

But I am convinced
that Athanasius smuggled grain.

Traces

There is so little left.
Of dogs for example
only their collars.
Normally sent home in an envelope
along with the bill
from the vet.
Of the really great writers
some extracts in anthologies
that are soon thinned out
over a couple of decades
and die away in the ever-shorter footnotes
of secondary literature as the century passes.
Of Admiral Dönitz, Admiral Nimitz
and Admiral Tirpitz?
A few rectangles and triangles.
Some red. Some blue.

And die away like a storm wind in the desert

During a long ride through the Chisos mountains
where the grit streams beneath the horse's hooves
and the canyon swallow, my friend among swallows,
sails silently
through space and time
I thought I could hear through last year's grass
the faint whispering of the gods
of the Apaches and Comanches.
(BIZARRE FIGURES,
ANIMAL FACES EAGLE'S CLAWS)
Very lonely now
in their stray worlds.

Minor gods

Major gods, a Baal, an El,
defeat the Powers of Chaos in a heroic battle

(they think)
and then carefully erect their fortress

on the highest mountain to be found.
And then they sit there content

and watch the smoke rising, straight up or less straight
from burn-beating, crematorium ovens and coffee-brewing.

The minor gods, the small fry,
lares, gnomes and the little grey wise ones,

dig away in the autumn roots of the old ash
and send strange fungi

up into the light of day. They are lazy, languid gods.

But they want to have a say as well.

Letter from a joker

Those who don't believe in me
are sure to end up in the fires of Gehenna

Those who don't believe in me
can really come to grief

'Believe in Me' means:
'Believe that I exist'

But if I exist –
do I really need
to be told that this is the case?

And if – perchance – things
should be so bad
that I do not

I have strictly speaking
not all that much

to threaten with

Lost property

(Irmgard)

Dear friend, whom I once loved,
when I now chance to see your name
I recall
the iron crown of the Longobards
frighteningly aged and simple,
more awe-inspiring
than any object of gold.

Last seen in the cathedral in Ravenna.
That, too, a thousand years ago.

Sleeping with a cat in the bed

I don't know if I like cats
Dogs are more my sort of animal
Dogs don't lie as often
But it's nice sleeping with cats
in bed, somewhere down
in the foot area just where the toes
cautiously peep out into a nocturnal world
like watchmen on the wall
of a very old city
Sleep City on the Plain of Dark.
The cat then at a suitable distance
but in a kind of secret understanding
with the toes, these ten watchmen
against the dark, chaos, the void
and the sound of the distant train.

And the cat's sleep creates in me
a deeper sleep,
its way of curling around its
own centre like an embryo
gives a feeling of intimacy
yes, snugness, in this world,
as if it was
a perfectly natural place
to stay in.

Libraries are a kind of subway

The ingrained smells of libraries,
just as self-evident as those of subways

a smell of hot metal and oxidised urine

And libraries *are* subways
You often know where you come up

to the agitated life of the surface again,

but sometimes in a completely unexpected place.

Ramsberg's thumb

There was something peculiar
about Ramberg's one thumb.
I think a circular saw had taken
half of it.

He had built our stove
in '39 and it still works.

The remaining joint
had something childishly round
and defenceless about it.

Nature and unnature
at one and the same time.
Or nature's remarkable ability
to behave unnaturally.

Even today
I often think
of Ramberg's thumb

The girl

One day life stands
gently smiling like a girl
suddenly on the far side of the stream
and asks
(in her annoying way),

But how did you end up there?

9

The hare

One afternoon he was suddenly there.
Completely still between the lilac and the currant bush.
Precisely as in Dürer:
the ears longer than the head
and the underside white. Large gentle eyes.

Why did he sit there so still
frozen to an image in the afternoon light?
Did he have a greater trust
in us than other humans?
What reason did he have for it?

Much moved, almost flattered
I shut the door. Went back.
To my own doings. The next day
I found him lying
in a strange posture,

something between sleeping and embryo
outside the workshop door.
A few drops from the watering can
got him to take a few hesitant steps
as if he no longer had any credence

in the world and its images
It was the following day I realised
he must be blind.

It was when I found him
drowned and limp as a rag
by the landing-stage. What I had
seen as quiet calmness and credence
was blindness and nothing else.

'Nature is good' it says
On certain packets. Brand name *Spreadwell*.
Nature is good.
And how do you know that,
margarine hawkers?

Events on the periphery of a summer day

The trapped bumblebee
cusses and buzzes at the window
in a foreign language

The old coffee-mill
can't stop going on
about rationing and war

A splendid spider's web
has taken over grandma's bicycle
an Evangelii Härold no longer for sale

From the century-old bush
gooseberries, brown as amber,
and weary, fall to the ground one by one

It is – in short – late here on earth
In the wall-mounted telephone
the afternoon storm is already crackling

On the richness of the inhabited worlds

In some worlds one has confirmed
Riemann's prime number conjecture

In some worlds one extracts
lengthy confessions from ancient fungi

In a certain world the profound darkness
is transilluminated by wonderful talking stones

In quite a few worlds summer lasts
a century, and those unfortunate enough

to be born during the winter century
spend their lives sleeping

suspended in fur-lined
light-grey cocoons

In some worlds even this poem has
already been written and rejected

Mörten bears his name with silence

Yes,
the lake was a soft-spoken teacher

in a never-ending summer month of childhood
the bleak danced in the shallows

over the warm sand
the burbot was a shadow in the deep

everything was a connected whole
but not for me

and mörten, red-eyed from late hours,
bore this his name with patience

and was consequently called 'mört' – roach.

Those that swam were a different, alien race
and yet just as real or unreal as I was.

Where they could live I could not
and vice versa, the hook in the jaw

the cut of the mesh over the dorsal fin
must have hurt terribly

and they bore it with silence
the silence that is peculiar to this world.

Mörten bears his name with silence
and will never know who he was.

The lamp

Before the lamp was lit
we sat completely still

A crow's rasping voice
and a sudden scent of clover

with a sweetish warmth
through this rising dark.

Water, completely still.
The earth, also tranquil.

The bird flew
as close as it could

over its own shadow

And the bumblebee, faithful
friend of many summers,

crashed against the window-pane
as if it were the wall of the world

And the dive dapper
flew from lake to lake

It could be late
or early
in various lives.

It could be in a butterfly's shadow
In the shadow of any life.

All iron longs to become rust

All iron longs to become rust,
said the old metallurgist

It wants to unite with the air
sink down to the bed of lakes

Become red earth. Not only iron
longs for its disintegration.

Utopias subside powerlessly
and become rhetoric. Even

proud monotheism rusts
away and becomes pleasantly

teeming amoral polytheism.

Sharp blades
gleaming swords and heavy axes
never last eternally.

All iron strives to become rust.
Said the old metallurgist.

Varnish on an oar

The west wind blows.
The west wind, curious,
in through the open window
and leafs through an opened book.
Which then reads itself.
The varnish on the oar
dries more quickly now
and at least one fly
is always left there
in the hardening, clear substance.
Like a question from outside,
from crystal-clear, empty nocturnal space.
And the book reads itself
not without reflection.

Mirrorings and folds

The great Atlantic shoals of herring
are able to reflect light

like a sudden gleam of silver
against the underside of the clouds

The silver cloud of fish
just under the surface of the sea
becomes a mirror of the sky's low clouds.

Traditional Dutch fishermen
saw it and learnt how to follow the shoals

through their reflection in the clouds.
An agitated light that moves

from one place to the next.
And someone asleep wakes up far too early,

And sees at this instant something silver
spreading towards wakefulness' heavy clouds.

From a hand-plane's recollections

Beneath the surface of things
nothing else is concealed

than the surface of things
As long as something

of the surface is left
there is surface. Nothing else.

The Christmas tree's visit

Better than a house in the forest
is a very small forest in the house.

A brief visit that ends fatally.
Carefully. Not a twig

may be broken underfoot.
No birds to be heard. And joy?

A forgotten
bauble of deep-blue glass
found under the lowest branch.

The prime numbers

The first ones
are dark fortresses

that were built by princes
in a long-forgotten age

They lie close to each other
and cast long shadows,

the land around them is a flat
wetland, hard to defend

They are built of a type of stone
no time can crumble

and all of the others are municipalities

that squat all around them.
They then get increasingly rare;

one has to ride far over vast plains
to see yet another on the horizon.

The truth is they become fewer and fewer

on their way to the fathomless depths

And Doctor Riemann's shadow stands, –
unnaturally tall and menacing,

in an endless sunset

Passing through dark regions

This is a sphere that has

a constantly expanding inside.
But no outside.
Such spheres exist.

I am the only one.

Through the looking glass

Dearest
sleeping so far from each other
we even so share the night

And we dream each other
If I woke up now
I would not exist.

I dream You
who dream me.

If I wake you up
I will disappear.

The meteorite at the Museum of Natural History

Large like a well-filled sack of potatoes
this heavenly lump of iron rests

in the peace of the museum. Its surface folded
in a way that inevitably reminds one

of an exposed human brain
it has something old-fashioned about it.

It existed before this planetary system.
Finally found in Greenland,

it was on its way to this earth
long before this world came into being.

Fearlessly falling through
the vast the most bottomless realms of darkness

arrow-tip ploughshare like an instant finally
turned into a sword that blazed, unseen by eyes

in the Cambrian night when it became our guest.

And when I, someone highly random, now
an instant later allow my fingers to glide

over this unresponsive, strangely still surface,
this far too experienced drop from the depths,

it seems, silent and wise,
only to radiate a distracted politeness.

To the knowing

The church of San Clemente in Rome
During the baroque with its swollen
rhetoric that shows that all yet doubt,
a floor lower down
the ancient Christian church
dark, cramped without adornments
with sarcophagi in narrow passages
a secret society of the faithful
who knew how all things stand
and yet another layer down
through narrowing stairs and passages
the Mithraic altar, meal venue for
a secret society of the faithful
who knew how all things stand

Trivial pieces of knowledge

Olive oil is a splendid agent
for removing rust.

Individual events lack probability.
They are point-formed.

Thus
I lack probability too.

The dead do not know
that they have ever existed.

Time cannot have begun with the universe.
Time cannot have a beginning.

For a beginning is always an event.

Horses find it very hard to sleep
if they are left out alone at night.

Horses watch over each other's sleep.

People with a disturbed mother relationship
become poets.

People with a disturbed father relationship
become tedious.

Spring's joyous choir of birds

(dedicated to Staffan Söderblom)

Ah those joyous voices of birds in spring!
How well I too remember the choir
of those small wingèd singers

They were borne in on a special tray
by schoolmaster Gustav Edin,
extremely dusty, increasingly pale in colour
and – it might possibly seem –

somewhat overambitiously
stuffed:
sparrow and nightingale, hawk and pied flycatcher,
meadow pipit and dipper –

And from a gramophone record
from Radio Sweden, much over-used,
all their joyous voices were played

I never learnt
to distinguish one chirp from another

And now in October the dull voice
of the curlew is all that is left

In any case
I did finally learn that one.

An early summer day at Björn Nilsson's grave

(Midsummer 2005)

Väster Våla graveyard in the light of early summer
and with the kindly southwesterly wind over

Brusling's meadows that must have been there
that mild morning in the sixties

when we invented the Monster in Bo Gryta.
The monster was a huge mol, and we needed it

to have something to write about in *Expressen*.
(It was one of those irritating weeks

when everything refused to happen,

world history hesitates or meditates
on what the next really lousy surprise

is to look like and no star had broken his leg.)

Bo Gryta is a deep-hole in the Åmänningen lake
to be found a few kilometres outside

the villages of Bodarne and Vretarne, on a line
between the former Boda harbour, where the wreck

of an ore smack that capsized and sank is said
to lie, though no one knows where, and Dentist's Point.

How deep is this deep-hole? Nobody knows.
Many have tried with plummet and line.

And when the line came up, snipped
just as elegantly as with a razorblade

or the chain they tried instead,
the cut just as shiny and neat

from what can only be
extremely large teeth, the attempts

were abandoned. Christopher Middleton
described them in his poem 'The Mol'.

This really had an effect:
for a couple of summers later a busload

of Englishmen, eccentrics and experts
came for the monsters of the deep. They sounded

and took notes. Per Brusling offered them coffee,
now an old man who knows quite a lot about the lake.

The summer wind passes over Björn Nilsson's grave.
And I'm afraid I am the only one left who knows

how it really happened.

The expedition returned
deeply convinced that this giant mol

not only gigantic and malevolent,

is also sly, extremely sly,
and knows how to hide in murky depths

whenever anyone comes there
in search of it.

In a cosmic August night

After a journey
that lasted two million years
the faint light
of a extremely distant sun
came to be half-reflected
in the steep mirror of a nocturnal wave
while the other half
was caught in the wise eye
of a roach which beneath the lake's black surface
slid slowly out of the picture
Ignorant of what it knew

Smoothness

Here now reigned the sort of stillness
that could be disturbed by a single stroke of oar.
The season that slowly cools.
The sound of a chain that is taken away
and placed on the bottom of a rowing boat.
And afraid of damaging the strangely
great calm of this mirroring surface
I kept my oar waiting in the air.

American typewriter

What I remember of that era
is the sound. It could
be like waves against a shore.
Single and melancholy downstrokes
or that cheerful clattering –
it picks up, here the water's darkened
by a sudden gust of wind.
I recall how at *The New York Times*'
Metropolitan Desk a lone Remington
could swell up into a cascade of downstrokes
only to fall silent just as suddenly again
It was an age
when one could still hear
people thinking.
How unpredictably thoughts come
and leave us again.
Like extremely self-confident guests.

Ramnäs railway community seen from the north

Nobody knows what year it is
Perhaps it is a year that has never existed
The road through the railway community
from north to south comprises the following:
Uno Hedlund's Cycle Repairs
where you can also borrow the phone
The post office with the unhappy lady who
naturally does not cautiously steam open
the station master's love letters
and read them with mild melancholy eyes
The district medical officer reserved and mulling
over the enigmas of the medieval plagues
in his white palace up there on the hill
The Co-op where the yellow buses turn
and where you can even buy kerosene
important for philosophical studies
That is why Fichte and Hegel still
have a faint smell of lamp-kerosene about them
The railway station with Clark Gable as a guard
('in this job, let me tell you,
you stand – all the time – with one leg in prison')
And the wonderful brass telegraph:
Trains out
The chemist's burned down later
the lady there was surly. To turn up there
needing something was an insult
she never forgave. Actually.
After which a bridge over Kilbäcken
a bridge that didn't mean much
Salholm's Grocery, the private alternative,
where the ham in the cupboard was always green
and the cheeses sweated like the peat-diggers
who dug on the bog out to the east

In Grocer Salholm's dense, luxuriant beard
there was always, while he served
the actually rather rare customers,
a lit cigarillo with the brand-name Tärnan
And yet he never caught fire
Here ends Ramnäs railway community
We'll tell you about the Church village some other time.

The logonaut

I have spent my life
ordering the letters of the alphabet
in various ways. Dealing and shuffling.
Into a reasonably long string:
a long ski-track across white expanses.
The alphabet in Sweden has twenty-eight letters,
And then the twenty-ninth
the empty letter between the words
Which has no name.
Like Zero it has no value.
That is why it is irreplaceable.

Lars Gustafsson is one of Scandinavia's best-known authors. Born in Västerås, Sweden, in 1936, he published his first novel *Vägvila: ett mysteriespel på prosa* (Rest on the Way: A Mystery Play in Prose), at the age of 21. He is one of the most prolific Swedish writers since August Strindberg. Since the late 1950s he has produced a voluminous flow of poetry, novels, short stories, critical essays, and articles, gaining international recognition with literary awards such as the Prix International Charles Veillon des Essais in 1983, the Heinrich Steffens Preis in 1986, Una Vita per la Litteratura in 1989, and a John Simon Guggenheim Memorial Foundation Fellowship for poetry in 1994, as well as a Nobel nomination.

His best-known novel – championed by John Updike – is *The Death of a Beekeeper* (1968). Previous English translations of his poetry published in the US include *The Stillness of the World Before Bach* (1988), *Elegies and Other Poems* (2000) from New Directions, and *A Time in Xanadu* (2008) from Copper Canyon. His Bloodaxe *Selected Poems* (2015) – his first UK poetry publication – is a Poetry Book Society Recommended Translation.

From 1983 he served as a professor at the University of Texas at Austin, where he taught Philosophy and Creative Writing, until retiring in 2006, and has held several visiting lectureships and residencies in Germany. He now divides his time between Stockholm and northern Västmanland, Sweden.

MIX
Paper from
responsible sources
FSC® C007785